T0357223

Spinout Ventures

Spinout Ventures

Transitioning From Employees to Entrepreneurs

Dr. André Laplume and Dr. Sepideh Yeganegi

BUSINESS EXPERT PRESS

Leader in applied, concise business books

Spinout Ventures: Transitioning From Employees to Entrepreneurs

Copyright © Business Expert Press, LLC, 2024

Cover design by Weird Wiring Studio

Interior design by Exeter Premedia Services Private Ltd., Chennai, India

All rights reserved. No part of this publication may be reproduced, stored in a retrieval system, or transmitted in any form or by any means—electronic, mechanical, photocopy, recording, or any other except for brief quotations, not to exceed 400 words, without the prior permission of the publisher.

First published in 2024 by
Business Expert Press, LLC
222 East 46th Street, New York, NY 10017
www.businessexpertpress.com

ISBN-13: 978-1-63742-575-6 (paperback)
ISBN-13: 978-1-63742-576-3 (e-book)

Business Expert Press Entrepreneurship and Small Business Management Collection

First edition: 2024

10 9 8 7 6 5 4 3 2 1

Description

For many aspiring entrepreneurs, the path to entrepreneurship begins within the walls of established corporations. This book is about spinouts—independent businesses established by former employees—and is specifically designed for employees and executives in the private sector. It caters to those who are either personally exploring entrepreneurial ambitions or dealing with them in their organizations. Whether you're considering launching your own business or managing employees with a desire for entrepreneurship within your organization, this is your essential guide to the journey from employment to entrepreneurship.

Delve into the choices that employee entrepreneurs make and the consequences they face. If you work in or run an organization, gain insights into the processes and critical decision-making moments through real-life spinout stories like Chevrolet, Apple, Zoom, Zillow, Intel, and Electronic Arts.

Spinouts have a distinct advantage, which comes from what they inherit from their parent firms. Their advantage hinges on what they absorb or carry forward from their parent firms. While some parent companies actively support and cultivate their spinouts, leveraging them to bolster their reputation, others adopt a more defensive approach. Learn from parent firm cases like Fairchild, Palantir, AstraZeneca, Nokia, and Paypal.

Explore the controversial yet often successful path of spinout ventures!

Keywords

spinouts; startups; business; management; strategy; entrepreneurship; self-employment; employee spinouts; spinout ventures; employee startups; employee entrepreneurship; corporate entrepreneurship; intrapreneurship; employee mobility; knowledge spillover; career choice; noncompetes

Contents

Why We Wrote This Book

Did you know that working for someone else is for many ambitious people a road to entrepreneurship and new venture creation?

This is intended to be an unusual book about entrepreneurship that is specifically written for *employees and executives of existing private sector (i.e., for-profit) organizations who are considering starting a business venture or dealing with spinouts as a parent firm manager*. Our objective is to explore with employees who aspire to become entrepreneurs the unique challenges and opportunities they may face. We also look at the spinout phenomenon through the parent firm management's eyes, covering some benefits and pitfalls leading to normative managerial implications. We cover what is rarely discussed—the relationship between the spinout and the parent firm, an experience exclusive to employee-turned-entrepreneurs and the parent firm managers that respond to them.

Nearly a decade of research informs this book, including studies on employee entrepreneurship or spinout antecedents, moderators, mediators, and outcomes. Early on, we observed that employee spinouts were not limited to just a few examples but happened in many industries and contexts quite frequently and successfully. The weight of evidence from the academic literature emphasizes that many successful startups benefited from a founder or two who brought something special from previous employment or used something they created or discovered while working for another organization.

What makes employee spinouts in the private sector controversial is the potential for departing employees, who start a new venture, to significantly impact the performance of their former employer's organization (the parent). Researchers have shown that a single valuable individual leaving likely is not much of a threat. It is when employees leave as a team that the most damage may occur.

We draw from a new stream of literature examining spinouts to shed light on the phenomena. Along our journey, we have interviewed dozens of employee entrepreneurs, ranging from those in the technology industry to professionals and those in other service fields. Using statistical methods, we have also analyzed hundreds of cases of employee spinouts involving noncompetes. We also refer to our literature review paper covering the employee spinout reality, examining over 100 academic studies on spinouts by economists, management scholars, and entrepreneurship researchers.[1]

The research helps to uncover a problem with the common narrative about entrepreneurship that is prevalent in traditional media and social media. Stories repeat the myth of the heroic garage or independent entrepreneur (we will discuss this in more detail in Chapter 1). Generations of prospective entrepreneurs indulge in the myth and may be led astray by it. We should not fail to recognize critical details in the founding stories of most successful startups, including how they gained something from their previous employers, be it ideas, know-how, co-workers, customers, or technology. Parent firms have an important role in shaping entrepreneurship.

Setting the record straight is important for entrepreneurs, parent organizations, and employees eyeing new ventures. Employee entrepreneurs often do not create something from nothing. Typically, they are not inventors per se but are able to exploit innovations they have learned from their employment experience. Employees also face significant barriers, including insufficient capital, hostile parent organizations, opportunity costs, restrictive covenants, and intellectual property protections. Yet, studies show that employee spinouts are more successful than other types of startups, suggesting that learning to overcome the barriers to employee entrepreneurship is paramount. We present short cases of several prominent spinouts at the end of selected book chapters.

Awareness and understanding of the special circumstances of employee entrepreneurs in some detail is important for incumbent organizations, too. A parent organization can differentiate itself as a place that nourishes innovation and supports employee entrepreneurship or one that is suspicious or hostile toward employee entrepreneurship, especially

---

[1] S. Yeganegi, P. Dass, and A.O. Laplume. 2022 "Reviewing the Employee Spinout Literature: A Cross-Disciplinary Approach," *Journal of Economic Surveys* [Preprint]. https://doi.org/10.1111/joes.12540

employee spinouts. A more benevolent disposition has many advantages that we discuss, using examples like Nokia, AstraZeneca, and Palantir. Ideally, we hope this book helps employee entrepreneurs and their parent firm managers to better deal with this exciting and challenging phenomenon (spinout ventures). We present short cases of the differing attitudes of parent organizations, their approaches, and how they manage their relationship with spinouts.

Summary of Chapters

Chapter 1 sets the stage for a book about *employee entrepreneurship* by examining the types of employee entrepreneurship, defining the book's terminology, and then prying at the myth of garage entrepreneurship. We look at the evidence for the prevalence of spinouts and illuminate the sources of their higher potential for success compared to other types of startups. We end the chapter with our first case study, that of Apple.

Chapter 2 covers a few key aspects about *employee turned entrepreneurs*, specifically examining the characteristics and motivations of spinout founders. We discuss economic rationales for spinouts, ownership benefits, and other motivations. We end the chapter with a brief case study of Zoom.

Chapter 3 is about the *causes and triggers* of spinouts, including the influences of strategic disagreements, managerial frictions, ethical issues, bureaucracy, and structures. We highlight liquidity events, mergers and acquisitions, initial public offerings, and downsizing. We finish the chapter with a case study of PayPal as a parent firm.

Chapter 4 focuses on *spinout creation process* and looks at what spinouts take with them from parent firms and who leaves with them. It also examines how spinouts raise funds. We present two case studies, Intel and Electronic Arts.

Chapter 5 introduces the *enablers* of spinouts, including the importance of learning environments, spinout-friendly parent organizations, and conducive institutions. The chapter ends with two parent firm cases, Palantir and Nokia.

Chapter 6 is about the *benefits and challenges for parent organizations*, including the possibility of knowledge spillbacks that benefit parent organizations. We also discuss the acquisition of spinouts, the benefits of developing a reputation for incubation, and the value of corporate cohesion. We present the cases of AstraZeneca and Fairchild to highlight key points.

Chapter 7 covers *spinout challenges*, including opportunity costs, work–life balance, restrictive covenants, fiduciary duties, chilling effects, and intellectual property rights. By being upfront with the realities of employee entrepreneurship, we hope to paint a balanced image of the phenomenon and the potential opportunities it represents. It ends with the story of Kik.

Chapter 8 discusses *spinout fallout*, the instigators of spinouts and the possibility of legal and reputational consequences of a failure. We add this chapter again to bring realism to this endeavor. There are potential negative consequences to be considered. We use the case of Chevrolet to highlight some of these issues.

Chapter 9 is about navigating *alternatives* and entrepreneurial decisions. This chapter covers the standard approaches of acquiescing, compromising, and avoiding as responses to institutional pressures. These generic responses may manifest as variations, including intrapreneurship, corporate spinoffs, intra-industry, and vertical spinouts. Zillow and 23andMe provide case studies to highlight some of these options.

Chapter 10 covers *spinout validation* and connects with the existing literature on the business model canvas and the practice of customer discovery. It shows how spinout founders may bring a partially completed canvas along with them.

Acknowledgments

So many people informed this book that it would be impossible to name them all. But we would be remiss if we did not acknowledge the spinout founders we interviewed, who gave us a trove of relevant and helpful quotes and the many researchers whose interesting articles on spinouts were published in leading management journals, capturing our attention. We wish to thank the reviewers who took the time to critique our related manuscripts. We also received generous feedback on the book from several colleagues and friends.

We wish to acknowledge and thank all of the colleagues who provided feedback and advice: Dr. Naima Cherchem, Dr. Parshotam Dass, Dr. Brad Poulos, Dr. Mohammad Keyhani, Dr. Howard Lin, Dr. Oleksiy Osiyevskyy, Dr. Scott Shane, Dr. Dave Valliere, and Dr. Sean Wise.

We acknowledge the help of graduate students and research assistants who helped along the way, including Bradley Bernard, Ataollah Taleghani, Fatemeh Yahyaeinejad, and Yu Wei Ye.

We also thank John Laplume for many helpful comments and turns of phrase.

CHAPTER 1

Employee Entrepreneurship

Essential realities are identified in this chapter. We explain the terminology around employee entrepreneurship, including the different types of related startup ventures and protagonists in the context of capitalism (see Table 1.1). We emphasize the importance of spinout independence, a key criterion differentiating employee spinouts from other types of startups. Next, we try to debunk the ongoing and inappropriate myth of garage entrepreneurship. Finally, we highlight the prevalence of spinouts and their propensity for high performance.

Types of Employee Entrepreneurship

A general term used in this book is *employee entrepreneurship*, which involves employees who develop new ventures either inside or outside existing organizations.

When employees, including executives, are developing new ventures inside their employing organizations, they are called *intrapreneurs*, the process is called *corporate entrepreneurship*, and their ventures are referred to as *internal corporate ventures*. As such ventures are carried out internally, they are thus owned and controlled by the employer. Intrapreneurs remain employees of the company but act entrepreneurially on behalf of and for the company's benefit.

When *employee entrepreneurs* leave their employer to start their own companies outside the *parent organization*, they are called *spinout founders* and their ventures are referred to as *employee spinouts* (i.e., independent startups created by former employees of incumbent organizations). They are called *spinout ringleaders* if they start recruiting co-workers for their spinout before leaving employment. If they are working on their startup on the side (outside the workplace) while employed, they are called *hybrid entrepreneurs.*

Table 1.1 Definition of key terms

Terminology	Definition
De novo startup	A new venture with no relation to a parent organization.
Parent organization	The organization whose former employee(s) are startup founders.
Employee spinout (or spinout)	An independent new venture created by ex-employees of an incumbent.
Spinout ringleader	Employee who recruits other parent employees for their spinout while still in employment.
Employee entrepreneur	Employee of an organization who starts a new venture inside or outside the organization.
Intrapreneur	Employee who starts a business inside of an incumbent organization.
Spinout founder	Ex-employee who founded or cofounded a business outside of an existing organization.
Hybrid entrepreneur	An employee who stays in employment while starting a new venture on the side.
Intra-industry spinout	An employee spinout in the same industry as the parent.
Inter-industry spinout	An employee spinout in a different industry than the parent.
Vertical spinout	An employee spinout in its parent firm's upstream or downstream industry.
User industry spinout	An employee spinout in its parent firm's downstream industry.
Supplier industry spinout	An employee spinout in its parent firm's upstream industry.
Private sector spinout (spinout)	An employee spinout that comes from a private sector firm.
Academic spinout	A startup that commercializes university technology.
Public sector spinout	A startup that commercializes government technology.
Corporate entrepreneurship	The process of developing new businesses, products, or services within an existing organization.
Corporate spinoff	A division of an incumbent corporation that becomes its own separate legal entity.
Corporate splitoff	When an organization creates new divisions under a new umbrella company.
Internal corporate venture	The startups that intrapreneurs create within their parent organizations.

Spinouts can occur either in the same industry or in a different industry. *Intra-industry spinout* founders start a new business in the same industry as their parents. For example, Zoom, founded by an ex-employee of Cisco's WebEx and very similar to Cisco's tool since both offer consumer video calls, illustrates an intra-industry spinout. Chevrolet,[1] a spinout from General Motors (GM) that made smaller cars, still competed indirectly with GM's larger cars. They went after a different customer segment but in the same auto industry.

By contrast, an *inter-industry spinout* happens when employees leave to start a company in an industry distinct from their parent organization.[2] For instance, a computer engineer leaves a manufacturing company to start an online accounting firm. The case of 23andMe[3] is instructive. The founder, Anne Wojcicki, worked as an investment analyst specializing in pharmaceutical companies. Her venture is an inter-industry spinout that does not compete with her previous employer; she was working for an investment firm researching biotech startups when she left to create her own biotech company.

A related type of inter-industry spinout is the *vertical spinout*, which happens when the alums start a new venture in the upstream (supplier-side) or downstream (customer-side) industry of their parent business.[4] When a spinout enters the industry of the parent's suppliers, it is called a *supplier industry spinout*. When a vertical spinout enters the industry of the parent's customers, it is called a *user industry spinout*. Vertical spinouts have great potential for transactions between the parent and the spinout. As you can see from the list of Uber spinouts provided in Table 1.2, a parent firm may experience a mix of different types of spinouts.

---

[1] See the Chevrolet case.

[2] M. Landoni and D. Ogilvie. 2022. "In Search of the Spin-Out Entrepreneur," *Journal of Open Innovation: Technology, Market, and Complexity* 8, no. 3, p. 106.

[3] See the 23andMe case.

[4] P. Adams, R. Fontana, and F. Malerba. 2016. "User-Industry Spinouts: Downstream Industry Knowledge as a Source of New Firm Entry and Survival," *Organization Science* 27, no. 1, pp. 18–35.

Table 1.2 Startups founded by Uber alums[5]

Spinout	Type	Description of spinout
Bird	Intra-industry spinout	Ride-sharing for electric vehicles
Beam	Intra-industry spinout	e-Scooter sharing
Kyte	Intra-industry spinout	Long-trip ride-sharing
January	Inter-industry spinout	Consumer lending
Mainvest	Inter-industry spinout	Connecting investors with local businesses
Xapix	Inter-industry spinout	e-Commerce software
Forward	Inter-industry spinout	Information technology for doctors
Gooten	Inter-industry spinout	Print-on-demand services
Evisort	Inter-industry spinout	Smart contracts
Kodiak Robotics	Vertical spinout; supplier industry spinout	Autonomous tech for trucking
rideOS	Vertical spinout; supplier industry spinout	Routing and marketplace services for autonomous vehicles

This book is about employee entrepreneurship in the private sector, which is distinct from *academic spinouts* (or spinoffs) as well as *public sector spinouts*. Academic spinouts come from university technology commercialization initiatives that are actively encouraged on most university campuses. Academic spinouts are usually encouraged by university stakeholders as a means of commercializing faculty and staff innovations. Similarly, public sector spinouts are an important phenomenon with very different conditions, incentives, and challenges. For example, national research centers like Los Alamos National Laboratory are known for producing spinouts that leverage government technology.

Another related but distinct phenomenon that often gets confused is *corporate divestiture*, including *corporate spinoffs*, where a division or business unit of an incumbent organization is separated from the company and issued a new stock ticker. The spinoff distributes shares to shareholders in the parent company. Corporate spinoffs are the result of decisions made entirely by the managers of incumbents. *Corporate splitoffs* are another related but different tactic that restructures the organization's businesses. This book is not about these distinct corporate activities.

[5] AngelList Talent. 2023. "11 Startups Founded by Uber Alumni That Are Hiring Now." https://angel.co/job-collections/11-startups-founded-by-uber-alumni-that-are-hiring-now (accessed March 2023).

Spinout Independence

Employee spinouts may be distinguished from corporate entrepreneurship by the fact that most of them are not sanctioned by parent organizations before launching as independent new companies. Generally, parent organizations do not have an equity share in the spinout, and neither the parent nor its investors are compensated in any other way.

It may take the parent some time before becoming aware of the embryonic spinout that begins its journey in stealth mode. The quintessential spinout creates a new legal entity (limited liability company, corporation, or partnership) independent of the parent organization. It is thus not a division or unit of the parent company. If the parent or its investors were compensated or given shares in the new organization, that would be a corporate spinoff, which is a different but related structure driven by the parent's top management.

For example, Palantir[6] has spinouts that are completely independent of the parent and its investors. That does not preclude parent investors from investing in the spinouts; however, Palantir shareholders are excluded from automatic ownership of equity. The parent receives no compensation and is either cut out of the deal altogether or at most has a license agreement with the spinout for technology it might use. In this case, the parent is OK with this because it paints the place as a great incubator of innovations.

Attaining independence for a spinout is sometimes regarded as a rebellious act on the part of former employees. Research shows that spinouts by former high-ranking employees and those involving large teams of ex-employees are most likely to harm the parent.[7] Parent companies bear the time-consuming and significant cost of recruiting and replacing the leavers. Some of Shockley's spinout founders were pilloried as the Traitorous Eight—a group of rebellious employees who left to form their own startup.

---

[6] See the Palantir case.

[7] R. Agarwal, B.A. Campbell, A.M. Franco, and M. Ganco. 2016. "What Do I Take With Me? The Mediating Effect of Spin-Out Team Size and Tenure on the Founder–Firm Performance Relationship," *Academy of Management Journal* 59, no. 3, pp. 1060–1087.

The Mythical Garage Entrepreneur

Mark Zuckerberg, Bill Gates, Steve Jobs, Mike Lazaridis, and Sir Richard Branson are examples of entrepreneurs who shape the public image. All of them dropped out of university when they found success in startups.

> While the romantic (and popular) notions of entrepreneurship conjure up images of a college dropout working out of his parents' garage on the next big thing, most entrepreneurs have significant prior employment experience ... and many prospective entrepreneurs first identify entrepreneurial opportunities at their previous job. (Chatterji 2009, 186)[8]

The myth of the garage entrepreneur needs busting. This myth is attractive maybe because it matches well with the individualism dimension of Western values. Young tinkerers, often geniuses, in their parents' garages or university dorm rooms create the next big startup out of bottle caps and spare parts. From an individualistic perspective, standing on the shoulders of giants seems less cool than doing it yourself from home. We tend to want to believe stories of rags to riches, even when they are cover stories. The underdog story is appealing because it allows us to dream of overcoming boundaries and obstacles.

Nonetheless, research shows that the majority of entrepreneurs come from established organizations. As a famous example, despite many people believing that Apple was a product of garage entrepreneurship, Steve Wozniak was an employee of Hewlett-Packard (HP). He left the company after he was denied support from HP managers for the idea of a personal computer that he was prototyping at his workstation.[9] So with this key piece of information that one of Apple's founders developed their first computer while employed at HP, we are left with a technology spinout story.

---

[8] A.K. Chatterji. 2009. "Spawned With a Silver Spoon? Entrepreneurial Performance and Innovation in the Medical Device Industry," *Strategic Management Journal* 30, no. 2, pp. 185–206.

[9] See the Apple case.

Many spinouts get a head start by using, transferring, licensing, or buying parent organization resources when they leave employment. Employees also learn from their time in employing organizations that can help them to become successful entrepreneurs. Organizations are like fountains[10] where employees can drink up the skills, beliefs, and values they need to become successful entrepreneurs. They meet new people in organizations and develop a network, which allows them to leverage resources for their spinouts. Organizations are also important places for entrepreneurs to learn about opportunities that might be available currently.

The Prevalence of Employee Entrepreneurship

It is salient to acknowledge the prevalence of employee spinouts. Statistics across industries and countries indicate this frequency. In a widely cited book, Bhide (2000) asserts that most of the founders he interviewed had the idea for their venture while working for a former employer.[11] Also, most venture capital-backed startup founders in Silicon Valley have prior experience working in other companies.[12]

Spinouts appear to be more common in some industries than others, especially so in high-tech industries like semiconductors and software. However, they are also studied in the U.S. automotive industry, Canadian service sectors, Italian tile industry, and American legal firms. Some prominent automobile manufacturers are spinouts, one being Chevrolet. Even Henry Ford gained early insights into engines when he worked at Westinghouse as a service technician. Subsequently, this experience contributed to his development of a gasoline engine for the Edison Illuminating Company.[13] Spinouts also happen in the retail industry, with

---

[10] J.B. Sørensen and M.A. Fassiotto. 2011. "Organizations as Fonts of Entrepreneurship," *Organization Science* 22, no. 5, pp. 1322–1331.

[11] A. Bhide. 2000. *The Origin and Evolution of New Businesses* (Oxford University Press).

[12] P. Gompers, J. Lerner, and D. Scharfstein. 2005. "Entrepreneurial Spawning: Public Corporations and the Genesis of New Ventures, 1986 to 1999," *The Journal of Finance* 60, no. 2, pp. 577–614.

[13] S. Watts. 2009. *The People's Tycoon: Henry Ford and the American Century* (Vintage).

Starbucks and Walmart being leading examples. Walmart's founder was a former employee of department store Ben Franklin.[14]

The semiconductor industry has been the subject of numerous studies of spinouts. Fairchild's so-called Traitorous Eight came from Shockley's pioneering silicon transistor lab. Fairchild is a spinout that became a notable parent itself, later sprouting many of its own spinouts. Semiconductor manufacturing is knowledge-intensive because the design and production processes are highly complex. For example, both Intel and AMD came out of Fairchild.[15] Apparently, intricate knowledge of the chip-making process is primarily obtained through hands-on experience. The industry is founded on several generations of spinouts, each using much of the same technology as their parents but often with variations.[16] Spinouts have also played a significant role in the disk drive industry too.[17] For instance, Conner Peripherals is a spinout from Seagate.

Spinouts are common in knowledge-intensive industries and human capital-intensive industries like software development and professional services. One can make software and offer many services from anywhere in the world and sell online to customers across the globe. Researchers have also studied law firms, given the prevalence of spinouts in this sector. This trend is particularly noteworthy because U.S. lawyers are barred from using noncompetes.[18]

Spinouts are well known in the pharmaceutical industry. For instance, pharmaceutical giant Johnson & Johnson is a spinout from Seabury & Johnson that took away 14 employees from that parent.[19] Today,

---

[14] *Walmart Is Born.* 2023. https://one.walmart.com/content/walmartmuseum/en_us/timeline/decades/1960/artifact/2366.html (accessed March 2023).

[15] See the Fairchild case.

[16] H. Lebret. March 2, 2011. *The Fathers of Silicon Valley: The Traitorous Eight. | Start-Up.* https://startup-book.com/2011/03/02/the-fathers-of-silicon-valley-the-traitorous-eight/

[17] C.M. Christensen. December 1, 1993. "The Rigid Disk Drive Industry: A History of Commercial and Technological Turbulence," *Business History Review* 67, no. 4, pp. 531–588. https://doi.org/10.2307/3116804

[18] B.A. Campbell, M. Ganco, A.M. Franco, and R. Agarwal. 2012. "Who Leaves, Where to, and Why Worry? Employee Mobility, Entrepreneurship and Effects on Source Firm Performance," *Strategic Management Journal* 33, no. 1, pp. 65–87.

[19] https://ourstory.jnj.com/james-wood-johnson-practical-problem-solver

AstraZeneca is preeminent as being benevolent toward its spinouts.[20] Spinouts are also familiar in the data-driven software industry; for example, Zillow was spun out of Microsoft's Expedia division. The approach used was similar to Expedia, creating a business out of data.

The frequency and importance of spinouts become even more apparent when examining their role in developing economies and forming clusters in specific geographic locations. Spinouts help form clusters worldwide, including in the Italian tile industry, Silicon Valley, and the Detroit auto sector. Clusters of geographically colocated companies are often the product of spinouts that stay near their parent organizations. Thus, for example, by banning noncompetes, California is encouraging cluster growth. Many other states and provinces, from Hawaii to Ontario, have followed suit, banning noncompete agreements to benefit their economies.

Although most spinouts stay closer to home because of family and business ties, some spinouts can also travel across the world. Flipkart is a spinout from Amazon that goes to India and becomes a parent there, proliferating many spinouts and forming venture capital networks to fund even more.

What does all this tell us about spinouts? So far, only that they are relatively common, bubbling up from entrepreneurial minds with prior employment experience at a parent firm. More importantly, as we are about to explore next, spinouts are a particularly successful form of entrepreneurship.

The Higher Performance of Spinouts

Evidence from studies suggests that spinouts survive longer,[21] grow faster, and outperform other types of startups.[22] Their competitive advantage over de novo startups is explained by the indispensable knowledge

---

[20] See the AstraZeneca case.
[21] F. Honoré. 2022. "Joining Forces: How Can Founding Members' Prior Experience Variety and Shared Experience Increase Startup Survival?" *Academy of Management Journal* 65, no. 1, pp. 248–272.
[22] Z. Cao and H.E. Posen. 2023. "When Does the Pre-Entry Experience of New Entrants Improve Their Performance? A Meta-Analytical Investigation of Critical Moderators," *Organization Science* 34, no. 2, pp. 613–636.

spinout founders gain as employees. Most studies comparing private sector spinouts with academic spinouts suggest the former have the business experience needed to exploit and nurture an idea. In contrast, academic spinouts usually have deep technical knowledge but often lack the business and industry knowledge and networks to make maximal use of their innovations.[23] Some researchers argue that the resources spinouts acquire from their parents may be the source of their competitive advantage.[24]

Inheritance

The mechanism that may best explain the advantages spinouts gain from parent firms is "inheritance." If we think of spinouts as the progeny of parent firms, then they inherit genes from their parents. These genes can take a variety of different forms. For example, spinouts may inherit business routines, capabilities, networks, and resources from their parent organizations.[25] Leavers go with the knowledge of the parent firm's routines that enact capabilities and make productive use of networks and resources.

Routines maintain the organization's knowledge and uphold its established practices. Enabling routines for spinouts may include how the organization negotiates contracts, conducts meetings, recruits, hires and rewards employees,[26] handles files, privacy, and media, processes transactions, forms teams, and protects its intellectual property. These valuable routines cross over from parent to offspring. Spinouts can also inherit business models and strategies from their parents.

Genetic routines may include how to access resources from stakeholders and use them productively, such as how to access industry network

---

[23] R. Agarwal and S.K. Shah. 2014. "Knowledge Sources of Entrepreneurship: Firm Formation by Academic, User and Employee Innovators," *Research Policy* 43, no. 7, pp. 1109–1133.

[24] E. Vaznyte, P. Andries, and S. Demeulemeester. 2021. "'Don't Leave Me This Way!' Drivers of Parental Hostility and Employee Spin-offs' Performance," *Small Business Economics* 57, pp. 265–293.

[25] S. Klepper and S. Sleeper. 2005. "Entry by Spinoffs," *Management Science* 51, no. 8, pp. 1291–1306.

[26] D.J. Phillips. 2005. "Organizational Genealogies and the Persistence of Gender Inequality: The Case of Silicon Valley Law Firms," *Administrative Science Quarterly* 50, no. 3, pp. 440–472.

connections and friends made inside the parent organization. Some of these relationships outlast employment yet remain potential conduits of information between parents and spinouts.

High-Performing Genes

Spinouts perform better than other startups, especially when they hail from high-performing parents. High-performing and innovative organizations invest in R&D, organization development, and human resources to generate valuable knowledge in technology, marketing, beliefs, values, routines, and social capital, contributing to spinout creation and performance.

Firms that invest heavily in R&D and new initiatives may make excellent learning environments for prospective employee entrepreneurs. Such environments are rich with learning opportunities, experiences, and connections to people who know even more. Steven Klepper and coauthor summarized the study results about the quality of spinouts by parent prowess as follows:

> One thing that immediately stands out [...] is that 22 out of the 25 spinoffs[27] originating in Summit County were started by founders who had worked for one of the top four Akron firms. While in part this reflects the importance of these firms, it is remarkable nonetheless because in other Ohio regions we observe a substantial number of spinoffs spawned by lesser firms. It is consistent with the idea that workers learn through their work experience, which includes learning from their colleagues, and there is more to learn at better firms. This impression is reinforced by the performance of these spinoffs. The 13 that were founded by individuals who immediately prior worked for one of the top firms produced tires for an average of 16.5 years and the other nine with founders who had previously worked for one of the top firms produced tires for 22.3 years versus 7.9 years for the

---

[27] In this and many other studies the word spinoff is used instead of spinout, but they mean ventures created by ex-employees (i.e., spinouts).

other 22 spinoffs in Ohio and 11.0 for all the other new tire firms (i.e., the startups) in Ohio. (Buenstorf and Klepper 2010, 110)[28]

Learning About Opportunities

Spinouts are expected to perform better than other types of startups because many spinout founders generate their business ideas while working for incumbent companies. This is a key difference between most spinout founders and other entrepreneurs. Spinout founders can conceptualize their future startups while still employed. By the time they leave their jobs, they have a more fully formed view of the opportunities they are chasing. For example, Durant[29] was confident about consumer demand in the small car market from the data he saw while directing GM. Similarly, Ted Livingston's vision for his Kik app was far greater than Research in Motion's (RIM), where he developed version 1 as an intern.[30]

The spinout's sharper edge may be the ability to leave with a more mature business idea rather than experimenting with schemes to see if something sticks. This is not always the case, though. When Electronic Arts' founder decided to leave, he was still developing his business plan when the idea and name of the venture pivoted.

Team Size

A larger team leaving a parent can provide the initial size or critical mass needed to be successful sooner, saving on the time and cost of recruiting a team from scratch.[31] Larger teams can transfer more complex knowledge from the parent. An optimal scale at inception allows a startup

---

[28] G. Buenstorf and S. Klepper. 2010. "Submarket Dynamics and Innovation: The Case of the US Tire Industry," *Industrial and Corporate Change* 19, no. 5, pp. 1563–1587.

[29] See the Chevrolet case.

[30] See the Kik case.

[31] V. Rocha, A. Carneiro, and C. Varum. 2018. "Leaving Employment to Entrepreneurship: The Value of Co-Worker Mobility in Pushed and Pulled-Driven Start-Ups," *Journal of Management Studies* 55, no. 1, pp. 60–85.

to gain market share earlier, rather than building it out over a longer period as the startup works to recruit its specialized team members from other firms.

Spinouts often have larger initial startup teams than do other types of startups, reflecting their ability to leverage resources out of the parent organization and industry networks. They are also better at attracting venture capital,[32] which allows them the wherewithal to hit the ground running with scale in all their business activities.

The initial team size is vital because in the early stages gaining market share is critical to success. In summary, not only are spinouts prevalent but they also have distinct advantages over de novo startups and academic startups if they begin with robust teams rather than a few individuals.[33]

Case Study: Apple Falls Not Far From the Tree?

One of the most famous spinout cases is that of Steve Wozniak's startup with Steve Jobs. Although many people may think that the first Apple computer came out of the garage, a better interpretation is that it came out of the learning environment HP created for Wozniak.[34]

HP is now a leader in personal computers and competes with Apple in several markets today. At the time of Wozniak's departure, HP was still making calculators. They had not yet exploited the market for personal computers.

Wozniak received an internship offer from HP's cofounder and president, William Hewlett. That is where he met Steve Jobs, and the two became friends.

---

[32] B. Joonhyung and J.M. Lee. 2021. "How Technological Overlap Between Spinouts and Parent Firms Affects Corporate Venture Capital Investments in Spinouts: The Role of Competitive Tension," *Academy of Management Journal* 64, no. 2, pp. 643–678.

[33] See Zoom and Electronic Arts cases.

[34] J. Livingston. 2008. *Founders at work: Stories of startups' early days*. Apress. http://www.foundersatwork.com/steve-wozniak.html

Disagreements

Wozniak created a microcomputer while working as an engineer, but HP was not keen on developing his concept further.[35] The management did not believe in the vision for an ordinary person to own a computer.[36] The diligent and devoted Wozniak presented his project to his employer, which was in the calculator business at the time. Wozniak begged HP leaders to make a personal computer five times, but they turned him down.[37] After that, Wozniak managed to get an intellectual property (IP) release and left the company.

Recognizing Wozniak's passion, Jobs invited him to collaborate in launching their own company, which would later become Apple.[38] Wozniak sold his prized HP-65 calculator and Jobs sold his VW Microbus. Together, they raised enough capital to build their prototype. They eventually got seed funding from Mike Markkula, an angel investor and a former employee of Intel.

In 1976, Wozniak, Jobs, and Ronald Wayne established Apple Computer. Wayne joined Apple to provide "adult supervision" and business knowledge but didn't last long at the firm.[39] Jobs managed the business and sales aspect of the project while Wozniak designed the products.

---

[35] W.L. Hosch. March 29, 2023. "Steve Wozniak | Biography and Facts," *Encyclopedia Britannica*. www.britannica.com/biography/Stephen-Gary-Wozniak

[36] M. Chu. 2023. "Before Apple Was Born, Steve Wozniak 'Begged' This Company to Use His Idea," *Inc.* www.inc.com/melissa-chu/before-apple-was-born-steve-wozniak-begged-this-co.html (accessed March 15, 2023).

[37] *Bizjournals*. n.d. "Wozniak: 'I Begged HP to Make the Apple I. Five Times They Turned Me Down.'" www.bizjournals.com/atlanta/blog/atlantech/2013/01/woz-i-begged-h-p-to-make-the-apple-1.html

[38] *Macworld*. January 5, 2023. "Who Is Steve Wozniak: Apple's Engineering Genius." www.macworld.com/article/670935/who-is-steve-wozniak-apples-engineering-genius.html

[39] B. Aaron. April 12, 2022. "This Apple Cofounder Sold His Stake for $800 on This Day in 1976: How Much Would It Be Worth Now?—Apple," *Benzinga*. www.benzinga.com/tech/22/04/26589263/this-apple-cofounder-sold-his-stake-for-800-on-this-day-in-1976-how-much-would-it-be-worth-now

Outcomes

Apple II was the first personal computer with color graphics and a keyboard, developed in 1977 by Jobs and Wozniak. The popularity of Apple II led to quick profits and soaring sales. The market value of the company hit one billion dollars when it went public in 1980, marking the quickest ascent to that milestone in corporate history.

Wozniak continued to work primarily for Apple until 1987. Jobs hired PepsiCo's John Sculley to be the president. In 1984, Apple Macintosh was introduced by Jobs. In 1985, Macintosh's failure to succeed as a business computer ultimately resulted in Job's ouster from the board by Apple CEO Sculley, whom Jobs had personally chosen to assist him in running Apple Inc. Jobs finally sold his Apple stocks—11 percent of Apple—and quit after being stripped of all authority.

Later that year, Jobs launched NeXT Computer Co., which Apple ultimately acquired for $400 million. Jobs assumed the role of Apple's acting CEO at the end of March 1997, following a $708 million loss and the resignation of the previous CEO, Gilbert F. Amelio. Apple quickly achieved profitability under Jobs' leadership, and by the end of 1998, the company had $5.9 billion in revenue.

Implications

- Firms may be unwilling to invest in the ideas of their employees that are unrelated to their core business.
- Frustrated employees can join up with outsiders to form a spinout.

CHAPTER 2

Employees Turned Entrepreneurs

This chapter explores some basic aspects of employee entrepreneurship, specifically examining the characteristics and motivations of spinout founders. We do not cover traits and motivations that spinout founders have in common with other kinds of entrepreneurs, like resilience, need for autonomy or achievement, passion, ambition, self-efficacy, tolerance for ambiguity, uncertainty-bearing, and risk-taking. We focus on how spinout founders differ from other types of entrepreneurs.

Spinout Founder Characteristics

Spinout founders tend to be more educated and have more experience, thanks to their tenure with their parent companies, often hailing from the higher corporate ranks. Here we consider how a person's standing in a parent organization affects their potential for becoming a spinout founder. Additionally, we explore how the nature of knowledge and work experience acquired at the parent firm impacts the potential for transitioning into a spinout founder.

Higher-Rank Employees

Managers, engineers, and just about any employee at any level within an organization can become an employee entrepreneur or spinout founder. However, research shows that higher-performing and higher-earning employees are more likely to start a business when they leave.[1] Rank and

---

[1] B.A. Campbell, G. Martin, A.M. Franco, and R. Agarwal. 2012. "Who Leaves, Where to, and Why Worry? Employee Mobility, Entrepreneurship and Effects on Source Firm Performance," *Strategic Management Journal* 33, no. 1, pp. 65–87.

role influence the potential volume of routines and resources transferred from the parent to the spinout.[2] Higher-ranking roles and positions usually come with greater access to stakeholders, which opens the door to resources.

Leavers are often clothed with their parent's reputation and, along with it, the social capital needed to get calls answered in the entrepreneurial context. With experience, they get to know who to ask for access to key resources, are able to make contact, and get a response.

Higher rank may make it easier to marshall resources into action to form a new organization quickly and effectively. Resources are usually available through a network of stakeholders, including employees, investors, suppliers, customers, and regulators. Higher-ranking employees typically enjoy status or prestige owing to the higher remuneration and power of executive roles, especially the CEO. They are also more likely to be boundary-spanning members of their organizations and sit at the table or on calls with internal and external stakeholder representatives.

> I guess one of the dilemmas any employer had how much do you tell your employees and how much do you train them to rise up and become a manager in that company or run that company, versus they leave and do something somewhere else.... There are two local professional organizations that I sit on the board of directors for and I still sit on the board of directors but instead representing my old employer I am representing my company, there are people that I call for to give work to or the people that I deal with on a weekly basis, they are all the same people and they deal with other people, other companies and other competitors of ours as well, it is just the network that we ran it, so actually 50 percent of people that I deal with are the same that I did in my previous employer, that is not clients, that's material suppliers and subcontractors. (Author interview, Founder 6)

---

[2] D.J. Phillips. 2002. "A Genealogical Approach to Organizational Life Chances: The Parent-Progeny Transfer Among Silicon Valley Law Firms, 1946–1996," *Administrative Science Quarterly* 47, no. 3, pp. 474–506.

Higher rank affords managers, directors, and executives a 360-degree view of the organization through systems, meetings, and reports. They get to see the whole value chain or "big picture" in a way that a contractor or lower-level employee might not. An example is ReNew, an Indian electric rickshaw conversion kit startup. Its founder, Srinivas, reportedly learned about technology leadership, materials procurement, manufacturing, and supply chains while working at Tesla in Fremont, California, as a production software manager.[3]

Managerial roles also offer a broader perspective on the organization's business activities, making it possible for the individual in that role to assess the strengths, weaknesses, opportunities, and threats faced by a potential spinout venture. One spinout founder told us:

> I got the opportunity not to see just marketing but I got to see how to run a business. Because I was at the executive table so you have CFO, vice president of engineering, vice president of manufacturing, CEO. [They] were going around and talking about running the company, and … I was very attentive. From entrepreneurial perspective I think not everybody is as keen to learn, but for me I took note of everything and I learned. (Author interview, Founder 1)[4]

Lower ranks often have compartmentalized duties and responsibilities suited to local problems, such as increasing the production of inputs to a business unit. Higher-rank individuals have a distinct advantage because they are better positioned to assess the value of the human resources they need to form their spinout. This can help them to attract the best engineers or other employees from the parent to the spinout. They are privy to information that many others in the company are not, such as the performance records or discussions associated with employees.

---

[3] R.N. Wangchuk. February 21, 2022. "Ex-Tesla Employee Trying to Make Indian Autorickshaws 100% Green," *The Better India,* www.thebetterindia.com/276627/ev-startup-zero-21-renewable-energy-electric-kit-founder-rani-srinivas-tesla/amp/

[4] All quotes from Founders are from interviews by the authors.

We should not underestimate the importance of ringleaders, who help coalesce a functioning team to draw from the parent firm. Spinout ringleaders learn to spot the key talent needed to create an effective startup. Technical founders may be more adept at bringing key technologies from a parent organization or replicating them in a spinout. Moreover, poaching may continue more subtly after the spinout founder's exit. Thus, a higher-ranking leaver's organizational knowledge and social capital make it easier to form a high-quality spinout team.[5]

Another group of high-rank employees are founder executives who receive a salary for working in the startup. Some may be driven serial entrepreneurs, creating one startup after another, even though such vigor is not necessarily beneficial for the first startup. Once a new business reaches a certain size, it requires skilled management to stickhandle the inevitable day-to-day issues that arise more than it does a charismatic entrepreneur. Some founders are unable or unwilling to transition into effective corporate managers, and their once-indispensable contribution to leadership becomes increasingly marginal as structures set in.[6]

Moreover, as the organization grows, so does the founder's reputation, and more opportunities become available to them outside.[7] Unlike professional managers, who are expected to stay on after the business' growth phase has passed, founders are usually no longer pivotal to the organization's success. Of course, there are exceptions—founders who morphed into great managers. Rather than becoming a manager, another choice is to leave the startup to begin a new venture. Founders are often in a better financial position to engage in another startup and already have the experience to do so. Therefore, it is not surprising to see many spinouts founded by serial entrepreneurs. Some flourish, some do not. Of note,

---

[5] R. Agarwal, B.A. Campbell, A.M. Franco, and M. Ganco. 2016. "What Do I Take With Me? The Mediating Effect of Spin-Out Team Size and Tenure on the Founder–Firm Performance Relationship," *Academy of Management Journal* 59, no. 3, pp. 1060–1087.

[6] W. Boeker and B. Fleming. 2010. "Parent Firm Effects on Founder Turnover: Parent Success, Founder Legitimacy, and Founder Tenure," *Strategic Entrepreneurship Journal* 4, no. 3, pp. 252–267.

[7] S.D. Dobrev and W.P. Barnett. 2005. "Organizational Roles and Transition to Entrepreneurship," *Academy of Management Journal* 48, no. 3, pp. 433–449.

when Steve Jobs was pushed out of Apple, a company he had cofounded years earlier, he immediately started a new venture called NeXT, which sold small computers but never generated substantive sales and ran out of steam.

Type of Knowledge

Research shows that most spinouts leverage the technical and marketing expertise inherited from their parent companies, encompassing both implicit and explicit knowledge, to introduce innovations in products and processes.[8] In the laser industry, "inside knowledge" or product-specific experience is essential to spinouts.[9] Sometimes, engineers play a crucial role in the spinout story. When the need for technical knowledge is greater than managerial knowledge, spinouts tend to be led by those in integral technology roles. For instance, Ted Livingston, a former employee of Research In Motion (RIM; now Blackberry), built Kik[10] while working as a University of Waterloo mechatronics co-op student at RIM. Similarly, when Zoom's[11] founder Eric Yuan left Cisco to build a new software platform for communications, he brought technological prowess with him—he had been one of the original programmers of WebEx.

As another example, expert technical knowledge about how to make microprocessors is what most Fairchild spinouts took with them, including Intel and AMD. While many of these spinouts were engaged in the production of computer chips, they employed distinct designs compared to their parent company. Understanding the manufacturing technology was critical as, without direct observation, involvement, and experience, it is challenging to replicate intricate, complex processes.

Technical knowledge is also vital at Tesla spinout Lightship, which aims to produce electric campers for outdoor-living enthusiasts. These

---

[8] R. Agarwal and S.K. Shah, 2014. "Knowledge Sources of Entrepreneurship: Firm Formation by Academic, User and Employee Innovators," Research Policy 43, no. 7, pp. 1109–1133.

[9] S. Klepper and S. Sleeper. 2005. "Entry by Spinoffs," Management science 51, no. 8, pp. 1291–1306.

[10] See the Kik case.

[11] See the Zoom case.

entrepreneurs first considered the electrification of food trucks but pivoted to campers after concluding there was a potential larger market for these products. Lightship founders include a Tesla alumnus, who was a battery engineer working on the Model 3 project.[12] Proficiency in battery technology would be crucial to enabling such a venture's success. Notably, the battery they use in their camper is similar, if not identical, to that found in the Model 3.[13]

Specialized technical ingenuity often requires more than one brain to be carried over to a startup. Successfully replicating a sophisticated process may require a team of leavers to work together, each bringing a key part of the necessary amalgam. Here, the significance lies not only in explicit knowledge but in the practical know-how of performing a task. Observational, hands-on experiences, and interactive discussions often contribute to a tacit understanding that might not entirely translate into formalized knowledge. Tacit knowledge involves knowing something without being able to articulate it effectively to others or express it through technical drawings or words.

In some cases, neither skilled management nor engineering is particularly important. Instead, sales and marketing take the lead. A strong connection to a major client can be a sufficient catalyst to develop a spinout. Even one big account can pay for the development of other complementary assets needed to be successful, making the spinout a supplier or another customer of the parent's supplier.

Ambidexterity Experience

Ambidexterity refers to the ability to do **both** exploration and exploitation activities contemporaneously. In our own research, we found that spinout founders were more likely to have recently tried **both** exploration (i.e., developing a new strategic initiative or innovation) and

[12] F. Lambert. July 14, 2022. "Tesla Alums Launch a New Electric RV Startup: Lightship," *Electrek*.https://electrek.co/2022/07/14/tesla-alums-launch-new-electric-rv-startup-lightship/

[13] "TechCrunch Is Part of the Yahoo Family of Brands." July 13, 2022. https://techcrunch.com/2022/07/13/meet-the-all-electric-rv-startup-steered-by-tesla-alumni/

exploitation (i.e., implementing a new strategic initiative or innovation) at their parent organizations before starting their businesses.[14] Thus, ambidextrous employees are better prepared to venture out on their own. It is not merely having a generic experience as an employee but one with workplace activities that mimic the entrepreneurial process that is most influential.

Some companies structure themselves to limit contact between their exploring and exploiting functions, leaving top managers to serve as the connective tissue. Their role includes sensing business potential from the work of those employees doing the exploration and transferring those opportunities to exploitation teams for implementation. Such companies make it rather difficult for employees to attain ambidexterity.

Fortunately, many smaller employers provide a fertile environment to grow potential entrepreneurs. Smaller firms typically allow employees to do more, see more, and interact with a wide variety of stakeholders. Often within large organizations, many employees are consigned to silos, departments or divisions with scant communication with other parts of the business they do not interact with directly. Still, even in large firms, another emerging practice is called "contextual ambidexterity,"[15] where organizations are allowing employees to do both exploration and exploitation-type activities as part of their work.

Motivations of Spinout Founders

It is often said that a person cannot win a game that they do not play. In the context of entrepreneurship, this statement suggests that success depends on people's willingness to become entrepreneurs. Moreover, because the pursuit of entrepreneurial opportunity is an evolutionary process in which people select out at many steps along the way, decisions made after the discovery of

---

[14] S. Yeganegi, A.O. Laplume, P. Dass, and N.S. Greidanus. 2019. "Individual-Level Ambidexterity and Entrepreneurial Entry," *Journal of Small Business Management* 57, no. 4, pp. 1444–1463.

[15] C.B. Gibson and J. Birkinshaw. 2004. "The Antecedents, Consequences, and Mediating Role of Organizational Ambidexterity," *Academy of Management Journal* 47, no. 2, pp. 209–226.

opportunities—to positively evaluate opportunities, to pursue resources, and to design the mechanisms of exploitation—also depend on the willingness of people to "play" the game. [...] human motivations influence these decisions, and that variance across people in these motivations will influence who pursues entrepreneurial opportunities, who assembles resources, and how people undertake the entrepreneurial process. (Shane et al. 2003, 257–258)[16]

These perceptive words lead us to ask, what are the dominant motivations of spinout founders? Let's look at economic rationales, ownership benefits, and health and wellness.

Economic Rationales

[I]nnovators may prefer to pursue their ideas in startups rather than sharing them with their employers. As the consulting company Ernst & Young put it in one of its reports, "Another risky issue is that of reward—a huge sticking point for intrapreneurs. Fed up with small bonuses and a few pats on the back, they often quit to form their own far more lucrative businesses" (Ernst and Young 2010, 24). (Zábojník 2020, 822).[17]

For some people, it is a basic cost-benefit analysis. If you are keen to look through a financial lens as to whether to undertake a spinout, the primary focus is on monetary considerations—specifically, the potential net return, including opportunity costs (what you could have done instead). Pursuing a spinout may be attractive if the expected net returns are greater than doing the innovation internally or not doing it at all. If entrepreneurs place a high value on maximizing income, they may seek to do spinouts that will be more lucrative than receiving a paycheck determined by someone else.

---

[16] S. Shane, E.A. Locke, and C.J. Collins. 2003. "Entrepreneurial Motivation," *Human Resource Management Review* 13, no. 2, pp. 257–279.

[17] J. Zábojník. 2020. "Firm Reputation, Innovation and Employee Startups," *The Economic Journal* 130, no. 627, pp. 822–851.

From an economic standpoint, what matters even more is that founders enjoy equity ownership in their spinouts—a luxury that parent companies seldom offer their intrapreneurs. Equity ownership has special appeal because the value of equity can grow exponentially as the startup grows. If a spinout's economic potential is great enough, it is more likely to attract investors, who may be willing to take a financial risk that could pay off in a big way.

Venture capitalists are fond of spinouts because these ventures tend to be closer to the forefront of technology,[18] having learned from their more established parents, especially if those parents were themselves technology leaders. One of Steven Klepper's strongest arguments was that the spinouts of leading parent organizations would populate the next generation of leading organizations.

Ownership Benefits

Yearning to be a company owner is a strong emotion in many people and maybe deep-rooted in employees who feel stuck working for someone else instead of working for themselves. Leaving employment to do a startup promises increased independence and autonomy. Here is how some spinout founders express the pull toward owning their own business:

> …we talked about me buying into the company instead, but it wasn't right for me. I wanted my own company, I would have left, and I was just honest about that. (Author interview, Founder 1)

> As I learned more about business and how things work within the company, matches and feeds the internal fire that I had always about having my own company, so knowing this you had to open with a franchise or something to have my own business. I connected the dots internally and realize this is a doable thing and then eventually pulled the trigger [and spin out]. (Author interview, Founder 6)

---

[18] S. Yeganegi, A.O. Laplume, P. Dass, and C.-L. Huynh. 2016. "Where Do Spinouts Come From? The Role of Technology Relatedness and Institutional Context," *Research Policy* 45, no. 5, pp. 1103–1112.

Benefits for Health and Well-Being

Working 40 hours a week or more for an organization can lead to chronic fatigue and burnout. While many enlightened businesses take employee health seriously by offering comprehensive health services insurance, employee well-being remains a concern. Otherwise, healthy people, who are overworked or work in an inhospitable environment, are more likely to become tired, clinically depressed, and suffer other serious health issues.

Recent studies suggest that leaving employment to become an entrepreneur may improve a person's health and well-being. Self-employment and entrepreneurship can allow better matching of work schedules to personal needs, thereby reducing stress. One recent study finds that entrepreneurs are healthier both physically and mentally.[19] More flexible work time inherent in entrepreneurship is particularly appealing because it allows for increased physical exercise, medical appointments, and healthier meals by adapting daily schedules.

Another interesting factor involves neurodiversity. Neurodiverse employees may struggle in work environments created by their employers. For example, schedules, in-person meetings, daytime working hours, and so on may be challenging or infeasible for people with ADHD or other types of neurodiversity. This makes entrepreneurship a potentially liberating pathway compared to traditional employment.

Case Study: Zoom Spinout of Cisco!

The Zoom story demonstrates how a spinout can quickly become a market leader. Eric Yuan dreamed of a solution to the solitude of his regular 10-hour train ride to visit his girlfriend back in his home country. The idea was to have a way to talk and see each other without needing to meet as often, thus avoiding the commute.

Yuan immigrated to the United States after several failed attempts. He came up with some of the technology behind the video calling technology

---

[19] M. Nikolova. 2019. "Switching to Self-employment Can Be Good for Your Health," *Journal of Business Venturing* 34, no. 4, pp. 664–691.

known as WebEx.[20] He worked on this technology as an employee of Cisco Systems in the WebEx division after Cisco acquired WebEx in 2007. Cisco is a top firm in the telecommunications infrastructure industry. They are also known as a hub of innovation and for making considerable investments in R&D.

Conflict and Opportunity

Acting as VP of Engineering at WebEx, Yuan wanted to develop a mobile-friendly version of WebEx but was turned down by upper management. He was unhappy when he realized that most customers were dissatisfied with the performance of WebEx. He lamented that the product still used his old code. Cisco was not interested in investing in rebuilding WebEx for smaller customers.[21] Instead, Cisco was prioritizing its Fortune 500 customers who could afford the Internet infrastructure to get a more seamless experience with other products.

Eventually, Yuan left to create Zoom, which entered an already crowded small- and medium-sized enterprise videoconferencing market that included its parent firm Cisco's WebEx offering and other players, including Microsoft's Lync and Google's Chromebox.[22] Getting investment for Zoom was challenging for Yuan, but he eventually got seed funding from another former WebEx executive, Dan Scheinman, who believed in Yuan's vision.[23] After that, WebEx's founder, Subrah Iyar, came in with an investment from his venture fund.

---

[20] D. Kent. November 16, 2022. "The History of Eric Yuan's Zoom," *News about Microsoft Teams, Slack, WebEx & Zoom (blog).* https://dispatch.m.io/eric-yuan-zoom/

[21] T. Huddleston. March 30, 2020. "Zoom's Founder Left a 6-Figure Job Because He Wasn't Happy—and Following His Heart Made Him a Billionaire," *CNBC.* www.cnbc.com/2019/08/21/zoom-founder-left-job-because-he-wasnt-happy-became-billionaire.html

[22] C. So and C. So. August 9, 2014. "Former Cisco Engineers Launching Alternative Video Conferencing for SMBs | IT Business," *ITBusiness.ca | Business Advantage Through Technology.* www.itbusiness.ca/news/former-cisco-engineers-launching-alternative-video-conferencing-for-smbs/50386

[23] "Zoom's Founder Left a 6-Figure Job Because He Wasn't Happy—and Following His Heart Made Him a Billionaire." March 30, 2020. *CNBC.*

Yuan also had to convince his family that the spinout was a good idea against the alternative of a stable executive position at a larger firm.[24]

Spinout Details

Yuan's spinout attracted 40 employees[25] from the parent firm over to Zoom.[26] This team included a marketing executive and a group of former WebEx engineers. Not everyone came all at once. Some joined later as the spinout's resources grew.

Perhaps it was Yuan's reputation and vision or the size of the spinout that did it, but Zoom attracted investments both from former employees of the parent firm and from others like Dropbox, which had put in five million dollars well before the IPO.

Outcomes

Zoom ultimately grew to such a size that an IPO was an option that could benefit early investors, founders, and employees with equity. It would also produce a cash injection that could fund sustained global growth.

The stock spiked during the COVID-19 pandemic as Zoom signed on many organizational customers looking to continue operations with remote workers. Zoom managed scale effectively. Zoom's stock price then deflated postpandemic as workers returned to face-to-face interactions.

---

www.cnbc.com/2019/08/21/zoom-founder-left-job-because-he-wasnt-happy-became-billionaire.html

[24] A. Konrad. April 19, 2019. "Zoom, Zoom, Zoom! The Exclusive Inside Story of the New Billionaire Behind Tech's Hottest IPO," *Forbes*. www.forbes.com/sites/alexkonrad/2019/04/19/zoom-zoom-zoom-the-exclusive-inside-story-of-the-new-billionaire-behind-techs-hottest-ipo/?sh=4b7604624af1

[25] Y. Weiner. July 10, 2018. "The Inspiring Backstory of Eric S. Yuan, Founder and CEO of Zoom," *Medium*. https://medium.com/thrive-global/the-inspiring-backstory-of-eric-s-yuan-founder-and-ceo-of-zoom-98b7fab8cacc

[26] "Former Cisco Engineers Launching Alternative Video Conferencing for SMBs | IT Business." August 9, 2014. *ITBusiness.ca | Business Advantage Through Technology*. www.itbusiness.ca/news/former-cisco-engineers-launching-alternative-video-conferencing-for-smbs/50386

The return to in-person life and work points to the limits of Zoom's business model.

Implications

- A spinout led by a technical founder can achieve market leadership by adopting next-level technologies.
- Dissatisfaction with parent firm leadership or investment can spur a spinout.

CHAPTER 3

Causes and Triggers

An employee may be ready to begin a startup but decide to wait for propitious conditions to present themselves. Of course, in some cases, spinouts may occur rather quickly, even spontaneously, due to quick decisions taken by individual founders, or even by happenstance. Maybe a person has reached a personal inflection point, suddenly realizing they know enough to become an entrepreneur and now view employment differently.

We have seen founders decide to take the leap following a serious accident or other profound change in their private lives. But in many cases, it seems the sole catalyst was the innovator's recognition that they knew enough to run a startup.

In line with the maxim that who you know matters more than what you know when you are connected to other successful people, their gravitational pull can be very strong. A surge in an employee's relational capital can also propel them to leave a job or become entrepreneurs.[1] Similarly, an entrepreneurial spouse may convert their employee spouse.

While various triggers are associated with spinouts, some are more common than others. We cover lack of fit, strategic disagreements, managerial frictions, and ethical dilemmas. We consider the structural issues in larger organizations that can motivate employees to spin out. We elaborate on liquidity events, mergers and acquisitions, and initial public offerings that can lead to spinouts. Finally, we discuss downsizing events where organizations abruptly lay off hundreds or thousands of employees.

---

[1] H. Byun, J. Raffiee, and M. Ganco. 2019. "Discontinuities in the Value of Relational Capital: The Effects on Employee Entrepreneurship and Mobility," *Organization Science* 30, no. 6, pp. 1368–1393.

Lack of Fit

Although a profusion of possible good ideas and innumerable combinations are available, most companies have finite resources and cannot chase them all. Trying to do so would put the business at cross-purposes. From a managerial perspective, not all innovations are worth keeping inside the company, and from a financial perspective, the firm should focus on its currently profitable businesses.

Organizations often generate many more innovations than they can reasonably handle. Some innovations are judged as being inefficient or insufficiently profitable for the parent organization. Some do not align with the core strategy of the firm (e.g., targeting different types of customers). Most often, the company does not have the wherewithal to invest in all of its employees' new ideas, while other investors do.[2] Additionally, the organization might lack the necessary complementary assets, such as specialized manufacturing and distribution, needed to bring the innovation to market.

Stage Gates

Large companies employ stage-gate processes to gauge how best to exploit their internal innovations. A typical process has a series of "gates" composed of panels of managers and consultants who assess and decide whether to advance or stall each stage. Each panel establishes criteria, for instance, potential market size or ability to reach milestones and meet benchmarks. A decision to continue, increase, or cut funding is based on that assessment.

Common stages include preliminary assessment, business case development, product development, testing and validation, and market launch, while the corresponding gates would be initial screen, second screen, decision on business case, precommercialization business analysis, and postimplementation review.[3]

---

[2] B. Cassiman and M. Ueda. 2006. "Optimal Project Rejection and New Firm Start-ups," *Management Science* 52, no. 2, pp. 262–275.

[3] R. Cooper. 1990. "Stage-Gate Systems: A New Tool for Managing New Products," *Business Horizons* 33, no. 3, pp. 44–54.

As innovations advance from small exploratory projects to new ventures with full-fledged products, more senior gatekeepers get involved, and the scrutiny intensifies. The objective is to pare down the hundreds of ideas vying for attention in a large organization to two or three best candidates worthy of greater investment.

The stage-gate process also aims to segregate those innovations that could do better independently in the marketplace from those that should be carried on internally or abandoned altogether. Part of the challenge is that many corporations require innovations to produce a rate of return similar to or greater than their existing core business offerings. This can be a very high wall to scale, especially because many of the most significant innovations—the ones that are industry disruptive—tend to be lower performing, at least initially, along some traditional dimension of performance and offer smaller margins.

There are many sensible reasons for parent organizations to foster most spinouts (see Chapter 6). However, from the employee perspective, strategic disagreements appear to be a common trigger. More recent research shows that other serious irritants, such as interpersonal conflicts, value-based differences, and frustration with corporate bureaucracy, incite employees to leave the parental nest.

Strategic Disagreements

Strategic disagreement was the label used to describe the root cause of spinouts by the late Steven Klepper, one of the first economists to recognize the importance of spinouts, especially in the development of clusters like Silicon Valley. He was amazed that spinouts were the highest-performing companies and that they came from some of the best parent companies.[4]

Klepper argued that because spinouts tend to stay close to their parent organization geographically, they are a potent source of regional

---

[4] R. Agarwal and S. Braguinsky. 2015. "Industry Evolution and Entrepreneurship: Steven Klepper's Contributions to Industrial Organization, Strategy, Technological Change, and Entrepreneurship," *Strategic Entrepreneurship Journal* 9, no. 4, pp. 380–397.

development. Spinouts often stay close because they are limited by their own founders' and employees' personal network ties. This, along with California's ban on noncompetes, made it possible for a major technology cluster to proliferate. If this contention is correct, substantial economic development may be gained from more spinouts simply by easing restrictions on employee mobility.

The grounds for strategic disagreements are numerous. Some are about business strategy, for example, a dispute about what type of products to target to particular customer segments. Others are about corporate strategies, such as whether a capability or function is better internalized or outsourced.

Strategic disagreements may also involve functional-level strategy (i.e., relating to marketing, supply chain, manufacturing, R&D, finance, accounting, customer service, or human resource decisions). For example, a senior executive may take issue with how the business is being financed, the level of service provided to customers, or the sufficiency of investment in human resources.

Strategic disagreements can be about technology strategy. This includes decisions about what and when to adopt new technologies and evaluating their competitive consequences. Choosing the wrong technology strategy has often been used to point out failures.

There are many cases of companies that invested in things but did not commercialize them. Mechanical firms that failed to electrify, analog companies that failed to digitize, and pharmaceutical companies that failed to genetify. Strategic disagreement about technology strategy is about the value of pursuing one type of technology versus another. One employee might want to continue with old technology while the parent moves to a new one or vice versa.

The model predicts the existence of two distinct classes of spinoffs.[5] First, a type 1 spinoff forms when an employee comes to believe it is worth adopting the new technology, but the firm does not. Second, a type 2 spinoff arises when an employee sufficiently

---

[5] In this and many other studies the word spinoff is used instead of spinout, but they mean ventures created by ex-employees (i.e., spinouts).

disagrees with the firm's decision to adopt the new technology that he is willing to invest in order to continue with the old technology. (Thompson and Chen 2011, 456)[6]

A spinout may be launched with a new technology that the parent has shunned due to its entrenched commitment and investments in older technology. Some of the cases discussed in this book provide good examples of strategic disagreements. William Durant saw the future in small cars, while GM wanted to stick with large format cars, so he formed Chevrolet. Eric Yuan was excited by new technology for video conferencing, but Cisco was not. Steve Wozniak wanted to make personal computers, and HP said no. Ted Livingston wanted to add many social features to Kik but RIM was unsupportive.

One contributor to a Reddit thread offered wise advice:

I worked as a professional photographer for a company that was film-based in the early 1990's. We had a good relationship. After 8 years working with them, digital photography became mainstream and it was easier for me to pivot (as a small, new company) than it was for them to pivot—considering their corporate investment in the old tech. So it was a change in technology, within the same service industry, that motivated my decision. After a non-competition period of one year (which I spent preparing to launch my own business) I sold to my first client in 2004. I have been in business since then and it has been great. Here is the lesson: I maintained a respectful relationship with the originating company (and eventually they also made a pivot and re-invented themselves). But now, today, a technology evolution is changing the landscape again, and opening new opportunities for both of us. I contacted the company and spoke with the owner and we're discussing how we can now bring together our two companies and adapt them to the new landscape. My advice to an employee who is freshly launching a competing business is to do it for sound

---

[6] P. Thompson and J. Chen. 2011. "Disagreements, Employee Spinoffs and the Choice of Technology," *Review of Economic Dynamics* 14, no. 3, pp. 455–474.

business reasons and maintain (if possible) a respect for your competition. You never know what opportunities will come and how technology or goals may drive you to find an industry partner. Burn no bridges. Respect your competition.[7]

Sometimes, the parent wants to adopt the latest technology, but that prospect may be threatening to some employees, who are not keen to change and learn something new or who may think the technology is a fad. That situation may cause a leaver to do a spinout using the old technology they are comfortable with while the parent company moves on to the new. In one case we studied in the telecommunications industry, the spinout founder saw there was still some opportunity in a declining commercial property landline business, turning it into a retirement pursuit for himself and a team of other former employees of the local telephone company. The spinout was profitable all the way down. They cut the business to the bone. They eliminated nonessential services such as cleaning, administrative support, marketing, and upgrades. Only basic maintenance and customer service survived, just enough to keep remaining customers satisfied and long enough to delay replacing their existing systems with new technology from the parent or others.

Managerial Frictions

Ever had friction with a manager? If so, you are not alone. A remarkable number of spinout founders report having been stirred by a bad relationship with their parent company management. A recent study[8] suggests that interpersonal conflict may be more relevant than strategic disagreements, at least from the perspective of the dozens of spinout founders

---

[7] *Reddit.* 2023. www.reddit.com/r/Entrepreneur/comments/1062ptf/anyone_leave_their_job_and_start_a_competing/ (accessed March 2023)

[8] S.K. Shah, R. Agarwal, and R. Echambadi. 2019. "Jewels in the Crown: Exploring the Motivations and Team Building Processes of Employee Entrepreneurs," *Strategic Management Journal* 40, no. 9, pp. 1417–1452.

interviewed.[9] Not getting along with the boss is such a common reason for separation that everything else seems to pale in comparison. Here are two respondents who reported interpersonal/ethical conflict with their managers as the main reason for leaving to do a spinout:

> Well, John [name changed] and I did not see eye-to-eye. One day I was in his office, and he told me, "George [name changed], the only two people in this company that matter are you and I." I told him, "John, you're really screwed up" … and I thought he was going to run the company in the ground and I said, "OK, I'm out of here." (Ringleader, 11)
>
> So they had a very bad way of treating people, and I didn't like that at all.… When you had a staff meeting … you would be dressed down for whatever little reason there was … it was a bit of a, "Why are you so stupid? Why are you so dumb?" All of those things were highly personalized. And when I was in my first role, I said, "You are in business with these other people. That's their choice. I'm out of here." (Ringleader, 9) (Shah et al. 2019, 1433)[10]

In the Netflix hit movie *Molly's Game*, based on Molly Bloom's memoir, a rooky gambling ring (legal) operator has a boss who is suspicious and jealous of her. He reduces her salary because he interprets her success at receiving big and frequent gratuities as making her too confident—which he views as a threat. This causes her to want to go off on her own. She solicits his best customers to her spinout by using his client list to text a new game location. All the players show up expecting to see her boss there. She convinces them to switch over to her poker table from then on.

---

[9] Shah's study suggests that the economic theories used by Klepper and others to argue that spinouts are outputs of greater external value than internal value were wrong. Most spinout founders value equity and autonomy from bad relations with managers.

[10] S.K. Shah, R. Agarwal, and R. Echambadi. 2019. "Jewels in the Crown: Exploring the Motivations and Team Building Processes of Employee Entrepreneurs," *Strategic Management Journal* 40, no. 9, pp. 1417–1452.

Her business goes downhill from there, nonetheless, *Molly's Game* gives useful business and life lessons for entrepreneurs.

Ethical Triggers

Ethical issues sometimes give rise to spinouts. For example, a company might be using a legal chemical that is also a toxic pollutant to save money. This concern could lead to a spinout that uses a greener approach. Employees are insiders, who are able to observe and perceive all kinds of potential problems within the parent. Often, when a stakeholder group is neglected by an organization, that leaves a vacuum for a spinout to fill by catering to those stakeholders in some innovative way.[11] Ethical issues may be rooted in pay differentials between employees that are regarded by some people as being inequitable.

A lack of distributive justice in an organization can forge the desire to do a spinout that values its human resources differently and treats people more humanely. The spinout becomes an outlet to make a better workplace while improving the well-being of employees and other stakeholders. A lack of procedural justice, where there is no reasonable way to have workplace grievances heard and addressed, can precipitate a spinout.

In the Hollywood movie hit, *Jerry Maguire*, which is based on a true story, Jerry is fired for distributing an internal mission statement about caring for clients' best interests over maximizing agency commissions. On his way out the door, Jerry is laser-focused on creating his own agency for professional American football players. After an impassioned plea (direct solicitation) in front of the entire office staff, he manages to convince only one employee, Dorothy Boyd, to leave with him. Spoiler alert: she had a crush on him. Jerry immediately makes a whirlwind of calls to his clients to persuade them to switch over to his new independent agency. But he manages to convince only one client to leave the parent agency and join his, the enigmatic Rod Tidwell. Jerry is not good at solicitation, but he

---

[11] A. Laplume, K. Walker, Z. Zhang, and X. Yu. 2021. "Incumbent Stakeholder Management Performance and New Entry," *Journal of Business Ethics* 174, pp. 629–644.

does manage to land a star player, who eventually becomes a beachhead for his new business, founded on the philosophy of caring deeply about a client's best interests.

A more recent example is Anne Wojcicki's story. She was disillusioned with Wall Street's exploitative attitude toward biotechnology and wanted the health care industry to be more prevention-focused instead of being what she saw as treatment-obsessed. She worked for four years as an investment analyst specializing in biotechnology company valuation. During this period, she developed the business model for a new kind of Business to Consumer (B2C) biotechnology company called 23andMe.[12]

A parent's equity problems can generate spinouts. If the parent's workplace culture and pay equity policies are poorly managed, it may result in some employees feeling unappreciated for their efforts. Employees expect equal pay for work of equal value and become disgruntled when they perceive unfair treatment. There may be whole categories of people missing from the organization's ranks because of these types of issues. Organizations purge themselves of those they discriminate against. While these problems can sometimes be resolved internally through the political work of insiders, turnover is likely if they are not addressed.

Disputes may flare up over the allocation of an innovation's net returns. Successful internal ventures may mean big profits for the company and fat bonuses for the C-suiters, but very little reward gets handed down to the intrapreneurs, whose ideas, implementation, and long hours made it all happen.

Environmental concerns now top the agenda for an ever-growing number of people, especially younger employees, who will be most affected by climate change for many years into the future. Incumbent companies that fail to safeguard the environment risk a number of penalties from governmental institutions, including taxes and fines. Some polluters choose to continue using older, inefficient, and dirtier technology because it is more profitable to do so. They might suppress or fail to invest altogether in greener technologies that could reduce the

---

[12] See 23andMe case.

environmental impact of their operations. This scenario gives a spinout ringleader plenty of fuel to energize peer interest in a greener version of the parent or seek to overtake it. When this occurs, the spinout is not only a hungry competitor, but it is one driven by a business ideology that contrasts sharply with that of the parent. Examples of this are starting to pop up:

> Former Tullow Oil and Petroceltic executive Brian O'Cathain has co-founded an Irish renewable energy startup looking to provide cleaner heating to big industrial and commercial energy users across Ireland and the UK. CausewayGT will focus on geothermal projects—where heat is extracted from the earth's core—and has partnered with oil services giant Baker Hughes to collaborate on projects and technology development designed to deliver low-carbon heating and cooling for commercial and industrial facilities. (Percival 2021, para. 1–2)[13]

Ethical questions abound about the proper and improper use of information acquired by employee insiders, especially when privy to company misdeeds. Some whistleblowers have had a career boost by going public with their criticisms of bad corporate behavior, sometimes even forming a spinout out of the frenzied media attention and venture capital they are able to raise. When employees have access to information about corporate wrongdoing, they have an ethical choice whether to spill it or stay silent.

Traditional journalism (as opposed to "fake news" newsmakers) relies on company informants to leak information about the inner workings that would normally be out of the public eye. There can be real incentives for doing the "right" thing. For example, the Internal Revenue Service offers cash rewards to individuals, who report tax evasion and other fraud, proportional to the amount of money able to be recovered—potentially

---

[13] G. Percival. December 21, 2021. "Former Tullow Oil and Corrib Executive Brian O'Cathain Makes Renewable Energy Shift," *Irish Examiner*. www.irishexaminer.com/business/companies/arid-40770648.html

significant cash that some whistleblowers can deploy to help them become entrepreneurs.

Working for an unethical company can catalyze a career change at a point where a person can no longer accept the status quo and feels that quitting the job is the ethical answer. The timing may be just right to start a new business, or at least a better choice than staying conflicted and unhappy.

A recent exodus of Twitter's employees due to what appears to be an unpopular leadership change may hasten a cohort of spinouts. We know that spinouts have happened in the past with the same protagonists in the storyline.[14] A recent headline suggests that a group of former Twitter employees are already trying to create a new platform.[15]

Interestingly, among the spinout cases we examined in the Canadian courts, several founders responded to parent company lawsuits with allegations and counter-claims of their own: complaints about bad working conditions (e.g., safety issues, lack of support, unpaid wages) or other employer misconduct like constructive dismissal.

Bureaucracy and Structure

Irksome company bureaucracy is another potential reason why employees may leave to start a spinout. Bureaucracy can make it long and difficult to get anything done, especially something out of the ordinary, like getting an innovation evaluated and approved for implementation. Faced with excessive regimentation, an ambitious employee may find it too cumbersome or practically impossible to do intrapreneurship.

Overreliance on financial forecasts by organizations makes them more likely to mishandle innovations. This is because new projects tend to be compared to an unrealistic financial projection based on the company's core business that treats sunk costs inappropriately. Evaluations are made

---

[14] M. DeGeurin. November 21, 2022. "Neuralink Co-Founder Unveils Rival Company That Won't Require Patients to Drill Holes in Their Skull," *Gizmodo*. https://gizmodo.com/neuralink-science-corp-max-hodak-elon-musk-1849808151
[15] J. Korn. February 13, 2023. "Twitter Is Stumbling. Some Ex-Employees Are Launching Rivals." www.cnn.com/2023/02/13/tech/twitter-competitors/index .html (accessed December 26, 2023).

with hurdle rates that are favorable to the current core businesses, the ones that determine today's stock price in the markets.[16]

Organizations have hierarchies, which inevitably means more people on the bottom than on top. Generally, there are fewer and fewer positions the higher you climb up the corporate ladder, hence limited opportunity for advancement through the ranks. Otherwise, the structure would resemble a cylinder instead of a cone.

Organizations concentrate power at the top of the hierarchy, though they may share some decision-making power with lower levels. Just as a federal government is responsible for international trade and defense, corporate leadership must take charge of allocating, accounting, and assessing resources. Just as many provincial or state governments have jurisdiction over public health and education, business unit leaders take charge of implementation and business-level strategy. Just as municipal governments exist to ensure public sanitation and operate local police forces, the functional level managers polish the products and services of the firm, confirm and affirm relationships, and exchange information with other functional levels as needed. These layers of management can present high barriers to intrapreneurship, prompting some eager employees to spread their wings outside the parent company.

Liquidity Events

Liquidity events make it possible for employees to access the capital needed to start a venture. Sources of liquidity include external investors, lenders, or the founder's own pocket. In some cases, personal savings may be sufficient to fund the startup in whole or in part. For example, each of Fairchild's founders invested some of their own money, and Electronic Arts' founder put to use much of what he had earned from owning lucrative shares in Apple.

Departing employees often need a source of income to bridge what can be a long transitional period until their new venture is making money,

---

[16] C.M. Christensen, S.P. Kaufman, and W.C. Shih. 2008. "Innovation Killers: How Financial Tools Destroy Your Capacity to Do New Things," *Harvard Business Review* 86, no. 1, pp. 98–105.

at least enough to pay the entrepreneur a salary or dividend. Interestingly, research suggests that an employer may increase compensation to incent employee retention, but with the unintended consequence that it better enables the employee to build up a cash reserve to launch an eventual spinout.[17]

Liquidity events are expected to relieve an employee entrepreneur's need to access resources for launching a startup and also diminish the financial need to stay employed at the same time.[18] Several organizational events can put cash into the hands of would-be employee entrepreneurs.

Many employees are also shareholders in their parent companies, either through stock options or share purchase plans. The former secures the future right to buy shares at a discounted price based on a stock's current market price. The latter allows the employee to regularly buy a certain number of discounted shares at the end of each pay period.

Employee stock options and share purchase plans represent compensation, usually over and above a salary and benefits, that is dependent upon the performance of the company as a whole. Senior executives are often offered very generous compensation packages that are tied to the company's stock price. The intended purpose is to reward them for making smart strategic decisions that will increase the company's valuation in the market. The higher the stock price, the more valuable stock options become. Stock options have a striking price and future expiry date. The striking price is set at a level that must exceed the company's current stock price, creating a major incentive for C-suite executives to drive the price even higher to make the biggest possible return. Stock options usually have vesting periods of three or five years, which is a temporary embargo on selling the shares. The purpose is to prevent executives from selling their shares too early in the game. The board of directors wants them to

---

[17] S. Carnahan, R. Agarwal, and B.A. Campbell. 2012. "Heterogeneity in Turnover: The Effect of Relative Compensation Dispersion of Firms on the Mobility and Entrepreneurship of Extreme Performers," *Strategic Management Journal* 33, no. 12, pp. 1411–1430.

[18] T.E. Stuart and O. Sorenson. 2003. "Liquidity Events and the Geographic Distribution of Entrepreneurial Activity," *Administrative Science Quarterly* 48, no. 2, pp. 175–201.

make decisions for the longer term that will boost the share price higher than the striking price.

Employee shareholders can eventually sell their shares, potentially creating a windfall that can provide the capital for a new venture. Other liquidity events are mergers and acquisitions (M&A) and initial public offerings. An early pioneering study found that regions with more IPO and M&A activities also had more startups.[19]

Mergers and Acquisitions

If the parent is taken over by another company via acquisition, parent employee shareholders either receive compensating shares in the new parent or are offered a buyout option. Typically, vested shares are bought back while the holding period for unvested shares is accelerated so that these can be sold as well. Thus, an acquisition may result in a liquidity event. But it may also nudge potential spinouts into motion.

A parent's acquisition can be an unfavorable experience for employees. The study mentioned earlier suggests that being acquired by a company in a different industry increases the likelihood some employees will leave to do spinouts. Acquisitions usually mean a changing of the guard as the new owners install their hand-picked managers to replace the current leadership. A full merger of both companies may involve decapitating the parent's senior management team, discontinuing most of the former business, and blending the remaining core functions into a similar or substitute product or service. Some acquisitions are friendlier, preserving the hierarchy and autonomy of the acquired business.

We provide a few parent company mini-cases, but PayPal's case is particularly interesting because it was precipitated by an acquisition. A majority of PayPal's original development team exited the company within months of its takeover. eBay's management practices collided with PayPal's startup culture, a clash that fomented many spinouts. Most PayPal employees soon headed out the door, many of them starting their

---

[19] T.E. Stuart and O. Sorenson. 2003. "Liquidity Events and the Geographic Distribution of Entrepreneurial Activity," *Administrative Science Quarterly* 48, no. 2, pp. 175–201.

own technology companies. Might PayPal have thrived differently had it remained an autonomous entity?

Initial Public Offering

Another way that employee equity is released is through an initial public offering (IPO) by the parent. When a company reaches a certain size and growth rate but needs more capital to continue expanding, it eventually becomes too big for even large venture capitalist investors to support. A public offering of stock may be the answer.

In an IPO, the company's private shares are replaced with new shares that can trade on public stock markets like the NASDAQ. Often, an employee's still-vesting shares are immediately vested as part of the IPO deal, allowing them to be sold right away. Interestingly, Pinterest recently allowed its employees to keep vesting their shares after they leave the company, reducing fears that the company might undervalue the shares at the time of employee separation.[20] Of course, one needs a market to sell shares. Often the internal market for private shares is illiquid, and the price does not reflect potential market value. In an IPO, employee shares become tradable on major stock exchanges, making it possible to raise capital for a new venture from the masses of stock market investors.

In short, some spinouts are triggered as leavers become flush with cash, bid farewell to their parents, and are able to capitalize their own companies. As with acquisitions, IPOs may also spur spinouts as employees come under increased stress from organizational strategic changes or new management.

Downsizing Events

Another type of event that can lead to spinouts is the somber prospect of a mass firing. Downsizing essentially pushes some aspiring entrepreneurs

---

[20] "Pinterest to Allow Ex-Employees to Keep Vested Stock Options for Seven Years | Insights | Overview." January 6, 2022. www.foundersworkbench.com/about/resources/insights/2015/03/startups-take-note-pinterest-will-allow-exemployee

by the threat or reality of layoffs or permanent loss of employment. As the risk of being fired increases, the risk associated with starting a spinout decreases. In one case we studied, impending layoffs were a motivation for the employee to quit and start a business using skills acquired while working for the parent organization. The respondent indicated in their answer to the question about whether they would have started their business if they hadn't been laid off:

> I don't think so, although at the back of my mind I had desire, but I was so comfortable there already, but when that happened it sort of jogged my memory and awakened that desire. They told me this is for three months and they called me even before the third month, I went just to help them out a little but I didn't want to go back there. I think if I was still doing what I used to do with them, I wouldn't enjoy it anymore and probably would be retired, but I still enjoy it. (Author interview, Founder 15)

Parent organizations might recognize spinouts as potential lifeboats for employees fleeing the sinking ship. Nokia is a great example of this.[21] Their bridge program helped many of their former employees to become entrepreneurs. We often call spinouts that leave thriving parents out of opportunity "pulled spinouts" and those that leave out of necessity "pushed spinouts." We might have higher performance expectations for pulled spinouts than for pushed spinouts, but not always.

Whether or not the parent tries to cushion the blow, waves of spinouts often follow significant downsizing by major organizations. For example, Blackberry's mass layoff in Waterloo, Ontario, led to a stream of startups joining the local incubators Velocity and Communitech as founders.[22] Some community-based incubators are partly designed as nets to catch laid-off engineers and managers and put them through startup training to help them form ventures instead of waiting for the next job offer to come

---

[21] See Nokia case.
[22] B. Spigel and T. Vinodrai. 2021. "Meeting Its Waterloo? Recycling in Entrepreneurial Ecosystems After Anchor Firm Collapse," *Entrepreneurship and Regional Development* 33, no. 7–8, pp. 599–620.

along. Incubators provide workspaces and technology, as well as business mentorship and ongoing training.

When Spotify laid off scores of employees after the COVID-19 pandemic, they offered severance pay. Instead of using their severance to tide them over until the next job offer, some employees used the money to build a runway toward a startup. For instance, one Spotify affectee was Stella Alexandrova, who used her five months of severance to develop her Mave travel app.[23]

Case Study: The PayPal Mafia

Some parent-spinout lineages go a long way. PayPal, the Internet payments company, began as an independent startup that was a rival of eBay, which had acquired a competing online payments startup. However, eBay eventually acquired PayPal, too, resulting in conflict with many PayPal employees and executives, who left the company, many starting their own ventures or joining others.

PayPal had nearly become synonymous with electronic payments on the Internet. It grew into a parent firm to several spinouts, with a culture that kept all these entrepreneurs working closely together.

Merger as Trigger

That cultural glue failed to keep sticking after the unpopular acquisition by eBay, which proceeded to impose its own values on PayPal employees. eBay's CEO John Donahoe was known to enforce a culture of high performance. A clash ensued between the freewheeling and irreverent culture of PayPal and the more goal and metric-oriented culture of eBay.[24] Freewheeling, according to Merriam-Webster, is "heedless of social norms or niceties," "not repressed or restrained," "not bound by formal rules,

---

[23] S. Bhaimiya. November 17, 2022. "An Ex-Shopify Employee Used Her Severance to Found a New Startup After Getting Laid Off With 1,000 Others. Here's Why That Can Be a Smart Move in a Downturn," *Business Insider*.

[24] E.M. Jackson. 2004. *The PayPal Wars: Battles With eBay, the Media, the Mafia, and the Rest of Planet Earth* (World Ahead Publishing).

procedures, or guidelines," and "loose and undisciplined." Irreverence is "lacking proper respect or seriousness."[25]

The merger with eBay precipitated many of PayPal's employees to leave the company, and many of them started prominent startup firms of their own.[26] Rather than retiring on their vested shares, they got back to work as serial entrepreneurs. Many of the firms founded and joined by members of the "PayPal Mafia" continue to prosper. Examples include Tesla, Inc., LinkedIn, Palantir Technologies, Affirm, Slide, Kiva, YouTube, Yelp, and Yammer.[27]

PayPal was eventually spun off from eBay but has not since been as startup-prolific as it once was.

An interesting trait of the PayPal Mafia is that they are not only founders but also include investors, who capitalize the founders. For example, Peter Theil, not only bankrolled PayPal, but he also invested early in Palantir. The existence of a network that includes investors and entrepreneurs who know each other's capabilities is startup gold.

Implications

- Changes in parent firms' leadership can trigger spinouts.
- A sudden exodus, such as acquisitions, can create a network of alums free to work together on startups.

---

[25] "Definition of Irreverent." April 14, 2023. In Merriam-Webster Dictionary. www.merriam-webster.com/dictionary/irreverent.

[26] R.P. Garrett, C. Miao, S. Qian, and J.B. Tae. 2017. "Entrepreneurial Spawning and Knowledge-Based Perspective: A Meta-analysis," *Small Business Economics* 49, pp. 355–378.

[27] T. Brehse and K. Kirschner. 2023. "Members of the PayPal Mafia Iinclude Tech Titans Like Elon Musk, Peter Thiel, and Reid Hoffman. Here's Where They Are Now," *Business Insider*. www.businessinsider.com/paypal-mafia-members-elon-musk-peter-thiel-reid-hoffman-companies (accessed November 27, 2023).

CHAPTER 4

Spinout Creation Process

What Do They Take With Them?

Spinouts are different from other startups because they are created using knowledge and resources transferred from a parent organization, often through networks. Therefore, it is relevant to ask: What do they take with them?

On the one hand, this transfer can take place while the founder is still employed at the parent as they acquire skills and idiosyncratic knowledge about technologies (e.g., products, technologies, processes) and markets (e.g., customer demands, distribution channels, market specifications), gains access to industry-specific social and financial networks, and discovers potential market entry opportunities. These endowments have long-term effects on a spinout's development and performance. On the other hand, the transfer can take place also after the spinout's foundation, when the spinout can exploit parents' networks, or benefit from parents' support.[1]

The process starts before leaving employment and it may continue for years after. There are various answers as to what spinouts take away with them. At the very least, spinouts inherit routines from their parent firms. This is why spinouts with founders from higher-performing parents are expected to execute better than those from lower-performing parents. The significance lies not merely in the types and quantity of inherited attributes but rather in the value added or enrichments derived from such inheritance.

---

[1] E. Vaznyte, P. Andries, and S. Demeulemeester. 2021. "'Don't Leave Me This Way!' Drivers of Parental Hostility and Employee Spin-offs' Performance," *Small Business Economics* 57, pp. 265–293.

In the most extreme or egregious case, the spinout could grab the core business of the parent company or unit. There are cases where the spinout founder is embroiled in litigation for allegedly "stealing" most of the parent's business or customer base. These circumstances usually involve former account managers with close client relationships, the local manager of a geographically distant unit that draws away the whole customer base of that unit, or a spinout founder that spirits away the parent's most profitable customer. In the TV series *Mad Men*, Roger Sterling's comfy relationship with a tobacco company heir ensures that client will abandon the parent to join the scheme for a spinout advertising company. While an anchor client adds stability for the spinout, losing a big client may be devastating to the parent's business.

In contrast, if the startup takes nothing from the parent, then is it a spinout? By definition, a spinout starts with something significant from the parent, at the very least a halo effect, but often something much more valuable: fully formed stakeholder relationships needed to secure resources for successful new venture creation and business growth. Between these two extremes, leavers acquire insights and knowledge in effective general management principles or gain experience in exploration and exploitation activities, which serves as valuable preparation for a career in entrepreneurship. Those experiences may have richly endowed the leaver with the ability to understand the "whole show"; the entirety of the business' operations and strategies with a sufficient mental roadmap to forge ahead.

In some cases, the prospective entrepreneur may seek to buy out a part of the parent company's business, license a technology from it, or enter into a supplier relationship with the parent, either as a customer or supplier. Vertical spinouts, as these are called, become partners in ongoing transactions with their former parents. They agree to collaborate rather than compete and simply carry on with little friction. In a vertical spinout, transactions with the parent may be a primary input and resource for the new business.

In one example we studied, the employee was an executive, who was in an accident, causing them to stay home for nearly a year while recovering. During that period, they conceived and started a new venture from their bed, selling a luxury version of the parent's products to wealthy clients under a new brand identity, independent of the parent's business. Rather than simply quitting their job, the parties negotiated an agreement whereby the parent would manufacture the spinout's products. This mutually beneficial approach is a model for others to learn from and perhaps follow. It is also consistent with what economists have observed as the fundamental role of spinouts to fill in available niches in the marketplace. One of the entrepreneurs we interviewed explained:

> We created a contract that I won't go to their space, I won't sell commercial, and they won't sell residential. They only sell to me for residential. Because they weren't really interested in that market, they were interested in me being interested in that market. They said if they wanna grow it they will go down a different path … and I had no interest in that, I wanted to do higher design stuff that I liked…. I was interested in this, so they were not going to pursue this but now I do it for them. (Author interview, Founder 1)

Of course, this level of cooperation between spinout and parent is not always feasible, either because of cost-inefficiency or it would change the direction of a spinout, impeding an independent and more promising trajectory.

In most cases, a single leaver on their own can carry considerable knowledge in their brain, especially if they were in senior positions where they got the bird's eye view of the parent's business. But some leavers try to take too much with them and end up getting into trouble. For example, leavers are often tempted to take client lists with them or e-mail themselves key documents or datasets. These activities are risky because they can be viewed as unauthorized use of proprietary information. In most jurisdictions, restrictive covenants and fiduciary duties limit pirated resource transfer.

Ringleaders usually need the specialized knowledge in other employees' brains, not just what is in their own heads. It can become necessary to coalesce and leave as a team when the goal is to transfer broad and deeper knowledge that combines into innovative business ideas. Complex knowledge may not be fully understood by any single individual. It may take a large, diverse team with each member bringing a crucial piece of the puzzle. Only then is the spinout able to recombine the pieces to enact the new business model.

Who Do They Take With Them?

We hired the three engineers [who] were the best guys [from the parent firm]. And it's like, well, of course they are the best guys. We are not going to start the company with dummkopfs. Of course we are taking the best digital engineer the company had and the best mechanical engineer the company had, and the best analog engineer that the company had (Ringleader, 5).[2] (Shah et al. 2019, 1434)

Attracting highly skilled human resources often begins while the founder is still employed, inconspicuously gathering information and stakeholder commitments ahead of their launch. Ringleaders are "originators and champions of new spinouts, and cofounders are recruited by ringleaders through a deliberate search process."[3] Ringleaders are looking for people that fit with their values but can also supply valuable know-how or access to complementary assets.

However, from a parent's perspective, a spinout may be an annoying and taxing cause of human resource losses that are difficult to replace. To mitigate the damage from employee mobility, several different tactics are used. Some companies have antipoaching agreements with each other to inhibit employee mobility. However, antipoaching contracts may run afoul of public policy, constituting a form of unlawful collusion in some jurisdictions because they restrict the upward mobility of huge numbers of employees. For example, Google and Apple once had such a pact, restraining the freedom of mobility of their respective employees.[4]

A spinout may attract soon-to-be ex-employees of the parent by creating new opportunities for employees to pursue. This may present an

---

[2] S.K. Shah, R. Agarwal, and R. Echambadi. 2019. "Jewels in the Crown: Exploring the Motivations and Team Building Processes of Employee Entrepreneurs," *Strategic Management Journal* 40, no. 9, pp. 1417–1452.

[3] Ibid.

[4] L. Whitney. September 3, 3015. "Apple, Google, Others Settle Antipoaching Lawsuit for $415 Million," *CNET*. www.cnet.com/tech/tech-industry/apple-google-others-settle-anti-poaching-lawsuit-for-415-million/

upward mobility route for managers and executives who have reached a career dead end within their current employer's corporate structure or had no leverage to get what they believe is a well-deserved raise or pet project funded. A spinout may also entice engineers who want to work on next-generation technology.

> [Spinouts] hiring co-workers from the parent firm survive longer. This survival bonus is greater in pushed-driven start-ups. We investigate two different mechanisms through which co-worker mobility may improve [spinout] survival—knowledge transfer and reduced searching costs. While both mechanisms play a role in explaining the survival bonus in pulled [spinouts], co-worker mobility seems to help pushed [spinouts] to survive mostly by reducing initial recruitment costs. (Rocha et al. 2018, 60)[5]

Ringleaders have been known to attract some of the best employees from their parent organizations, especially executives with a network of top-quality industry contacts that can access the complementary assets that spinouts covet—that is, who to use for manufacturing, distribution, marketing, and so on. Spinout founders also try to poach other employees, those with special knowledge and connections, yielding the kind of stakeholder-resource network needed for sustained innovation.

An organization is a network of stakeholder relationships that provide the company with access to the resources needed to do business.[6] Complex knowledge transfers are difficult to pull off because it often takes a collective of talented people in possession of all of the details necessary to fully assemble the components of innovation. A ringleader has the arduous task of creating a distinct identity for the spinout that is more alluring than that of the parent organization. A powerful vision is needed to

---

[5] V. Rocha, A. Carneiro, and C. Varum. 2018. "Leaving Employment to Entrepreneurship: The Value of Co-Worker Mobility in Pushed and Pulled-Driven Start-ups," *Journal of Management Studies* 55, no. 1, pp. 60–85.

[6] J.B. Barney. 2018. "Why Resource-Based Theory's Model of Profit Appropriation Must Incorporate a Stakeholder Perspective," *Strategic Management Journal* 39, no. 13, pp. 3305–3325.

attract a team with the right complementary knowledge and skills to put together the whole puzzle.

How Spinouts Get Financing

Spinouts may attract venture capitalists (VCs) if they provide direct access to the prized knowledge of parent firms. VCs can also be deterred from investing in spinouts from parents that are not spinout-friendly, being risk averse to any kind of legal conflict with incumbent firms. However, the magnetism of spinouts from high-profile parents is very strong indeed.

> In 2011, the benefit of having worked for Google is presumably that it tells people that you are smart and creative; the cost of having worked for an aging industrial giant is presumably that it signals the opposite. These assessments influence the entrepreneurial process, particularly in terms of the ability of individuals to mobilize the resources needed to launch a new venture. [...] Ventures launched by employees from "entrepreneurially prominent" employers (i.e., employers that have been the source of many entrepreneurial ventures) are more likely to pursue innovative ideas and more likely to secure external financing. [...] This reflects the reputational consequences of employer affiliation, because affiliation with prominent firms helps reduce the perceived uncertainty of innovative ventures. (Sørensen and Fassiotto 2011, 1327)[7]

Being from a prominent firm can make it easier to get the stakeholder support needed to form a spinout successfully. Investors, for example, may assume that a spinout from a top firm is more likely to be high-performing. However, for many founders, raising funds is still an uphill climb because most new ventures worth starting require a significant initial investment. If significant capital is not required, there are probably

---

[7] J.B. Sørensen and M.A. Fassiotto. 2011. "Organizations as Fonts of Entrepreneurship," *Organization Science* 22, no. 5, pp. 1322–1331.

too few barriers to entry in that industry segment, and the competition is likely to be vicious.

Like other startups, employee spinouts may obtain funding from angel investors, VCs, or self-fund their ventures. Preseed investments are made at the outset to pay for product prototyping, testing, or market research. Initial capital in a startup is usually called a seed (or preseed) investment, adequate funding to operate until the business is either self-sufficient or ripe enough to attract further investment. The next round, Series A, involves a consortium of venture capital firms that provide the funding needed to scale the venture and grow. Further rounds (series B, C, D, E) may take place until the firm is profitable or poised for sale or initial public offering (IPO).

Raising money by spinout founders tends to be different than it is for other startups. They are in a special position to get funding from former employees, founders, investors, executives, customers, or suppliers of their parent organizations. Founders commonly get seed investments from other alums. Ex-employees of the same parent are more likely to have access to information about the quality of the innovation if it originated in the parent's environment. Alums are more likely to know each other's reputations due to internal channels. For example, Peter Theil's Founders Fund invested in startups by many PayPal alums. Palantir's first CEO, Lonsdale, set up Formation 8 to fund Palantir spinouts and other startups. Also, one of Zoom's first funders was just such a case. One of his early investors was a fellow former Cisco executive who had faith in Yuan's venture. Another was the founder of the original WebEx.

Our research[8] shows that venture capital availability is positively associated with the likelihood that an employee from the core area of the parent firm will start a spinout. VCs are interested in spinouts because they want to invest in startups with the requisite knowledge and know-how to succeed. VCs are less inclined toward spinouts from the periphery of an organization, often coming after the replication of core

---

[8] S. Yeganegi, A.O. Laplume, P. Dass, and C.-L. Huynh. 2016. "Where Do Spinouts Come From? The Role of Technology Relatedness and Institutional Context," *Research Policy* 45, no. 5, pp. 1103–1112.

technology. VCs most value those founders who have direct, ground-breaking experience.

Case Study: Intel—Enacting Moore's Law

Robert Noyce and Gordon Moore were prominent innovators in the Silicon Valley tech sector due to their prior work on electronic components. A few years earlier, Moore and seven co-workers had quit their jobs at Shockley Transistors and started their new business, Fairchild Semiconductor. Moore directed development and research. Noyce was general manager and, in 1959, invented the silicon electrical circuit. Noyce and Moore then left Fairchild Semiconductor to form Intel in 1968. Investors Arthur Rock and Max Palevsky provided the initial seed capital for Intel.

Noyce and Moore implemented their entrepreneurial project as a startup around the strategy of continuous innovation in microprocessors. They believed innovation plays a key role in their new venture growth and long-term performance, whereas other organization functions are secondary and should be outsourced.[9]

Founder Background

Noyce and Moore had a problem with the parent company's strategy.[10] Fairchild Semiconductor was a manufacturer of the Fairchild image sensor and invested more in highly related technologies. The pair believed that the parent company would fail to invest sufficient developmental resources in research and development on new semiconductor technologies.

Noyce was mowing his lawn when Moore came over. The two started talking about the possibility of semiconductor memory technology as

---

[9] Intel. 2023. "Intel's Founding." www.intel.com/content/www/us/en/history/virtual-vault/articles/intels-founding.html (accessed March 15, 2023).

[10] M. Hall. March 26, 2023. "Intel | History, Products, & Facts," *Encyclopedia Britannica*. www.britannica.com/topic/Intel

the basis for a startup.[11] They raised funds from VC Arthur Rock, who invested $2.5 million to help Intel launch. Incidentally, Rock is credited with coining the term "venture capital" and hence "venture capitalist."

Resources Transferred

When Noyce and Moore left to form Intel, it was the "Fairchild Brain Drain."[12] What is instructive in this story is Noyce's explicit recognition that the creation of Intel would deflate Fairchild's prospects by removing much of its intellectual capacity. For example, Moore was credited with a folk law that every 18 months could yield another generation of chips that were cheaper and more powerful. It was not only Noyce and Moore who left; many other Fairchild alums followed them,[13] including Andrew Grove. Noyce, Moore, and Grove alternated as chairman and CEO for Intel's first three decades. Together they implemented the inflection points strategy, which posits that innovations always come along to change the rules of the game.[14] Their research scientists and engineers cooperate to help make dramatic changes in the company's strategy in response to market changes.

Noyce's mission statement and viewpoint were that every employee could significantly contribute to business improvement if they knew how to use their capacity and expertise. He believed that employees should not overthink the weaknesses and obstacles of Intel but rather capitalize on its strengths and the tremendous opportunity created by the fast growing semiconductor industry.[15]

---

[11] "Explore Intel's History." 2023. https://timeline.intel.com/ (accessed March 15, 2023).

[12] Chip History. 2023. "The Story of the Birth of Intel." www.chiphistory .org/713-intel-s-founding (accessed March 15, 2023).

[13] M.A. Dennis. March 25, 2023. "Gordon Moore | Biography & Facts," *Encyclopedia Britannica*. www.britannica.com/biography/Gordon-Moore

[14] P. Sherlock. 2023. "Strategic Inflection Points: What Is the Best Strategy?" Www .Linkedin.Com. www.linkedin.com/pulse/strategic-inflection-points-what-best-strategy-pat-sherlock/ (accessed March 15, 2023).

[15] Intel. 2023. "Wolfe's Tinkering of Robert Noyce." www.intel.com/content/ www/us/en/history/virtual-vault/articles/wolfes-tinkering-of-robert-noyce.htm (accessed May 4, 2023).

Outcomes

Despite its spinout origin, Intel was known to be unsupportive of employees who left to form competing startups.[16] Only later did the company adopt a policy of benevolence toward supplier industry spin-outs that could provide the components needed for production. Intel did not want to make any of its own equipment because it would be daunting to keep up with technological changes in many areas simultaneously.[17]

Implications

- Spinout teams may need to move complex knowledge and replicate capabilities.
- Resource allocation decisions can spur whole teams to leave the organization.

Case Study: Electronic Arts

Electronic Arts (EA) is a leading media company specializing in video and computer game software. EA has seen rapid growth and expanding global market reach.

In 1987, Trip Hawkins completed his education at Harvard and landed a job at Apple as Director of Strategy and Marketing. At that time, Apple's revenue was still relatively small, and the whole organization had only 50 employees.

He accomplished his dream by benefiting from Apple's IPO in 1980. Having abundant wealth from Apple's growth strategy leading to an IPO, Hawkins decided to start his own business.

---

[16] S. Klepper. August 1, 2001. "Employee Startups in High-Tech Industries," *Industrial and Corporate Change* 10, no. 3, pp. 639–674. https://doi.org/10.1093/icc/10.3.639

[17] B. Cirillo. February 4, 2019. "External Learning Strategies and Technological Search Output: Spinout Strategy and Corporate Invention Quality," *Organization Science* 30, no. 2, pp. 361–382. https://doi.org/10.1287/orsc.2018.1233

He raised five million dollars from private investors and used it to fund EA. After four years, its revenue streams had increased to one billion dollars per year.

Spinout Story

Hawkins was patient with his business model. He left Apple, and then worked hard on his business plan. He wanted to investigate the entertainment potential of personal computers.[18] He started to work on his new venture in an office provided by Sequoia Capital, his early investor. Hawkins quietly worked on his business plan for more than seven months.

His was a disruptive innovation strategy, wanting to transform television and radio into digital entertainment.[19] His core idea pivoted, but he eventually landed on EA, specializing in sports video gaming. Hawkins documented the initial proposal on an Apple II in Sequoia's office in August 1982.

Dave Evans and Pat Marriott were early hires who had worked for Apple. They were employed by Hawkins, as well as Stanford MBA classmate, Jeff Burton, who worked at Atari in worldwide product development. He managed to hire from Xerox and others from Apple too, with Steve Wozniak serving on their board.

Outcomes

Hawkins stepped down as CEO of EA to apply himself to 3DO, a new hardware platform for gaming that he started championing.[20] EA owns nearly 6 percent of 3DO, making it one of the company's major shareholders. More than 9 percent of shares are owned by Hawkins.[21]

---

[18] "Electronic Arts Spinoff 3DO Finds New Legs in Video Game Software." n.d. www.bizjournals.com/sanjose/stories/1998/08/24/smallb4.html

[19] J. Fleming. n.d. "We See Farther—A History of Electronic Arts." www.gamedeveloper.com/business/we-see-farther---a-history-of-electronic-arts

[20] Wikipedia Contributors. April 11, 2023. "Electronic Arts," *Wikipedia*. https://en.wikipedia.org/wiki/Electronic_Arts#cite_note-NGen11-13

[21] "Electronic Arts Spinoff 3DO Finds New Legs in Video Game Software." n.d. www.bizjournals.com/sanjose/stories/1998/08/24/smallb4.html

In the years after Hawkins' departure, EA expanded tremendously. His singular attention to sports video games was limiting the company's growth potential in other areas of gaming.

Implications

- A parent firm's IPO can trigger spinouts by putting cash in employees' hands.
- Building a startup with parent firm employees takes vision and leadership.
- Spinouts may need a period of stealthy incubation to find their way.

CHAPTER 5

Spinout Enablers

Enablers of spinouts are many, but we cover the learning environment, parent organization benevolence, enabling institutions, and open innovation strategies. These are enabling dimensions that overlap the least with entrepreneurship in general, where a search for enablers may often lead to things like reduced steps and time to create a new limited liability company, corporate tax rate, the presence of subsidies, or friendly laws.

Learning Environment

I think what was most helpful to start my own business was having desire to do it … at my old company I was stockholder so I did have permission to access lot of the projects information, like if it was profitable or not, what kind of clients were more profitable, so when I try to learn more about business I realized that was actually profitable for me to do. I was able to see there are projects that you make a little money on, and there are projects that you lose a little money on, and there are also projects that you make lots of money on, and there are also projects that you lose lots of money on. You just try to figure out what the right variable to put in the equation to have a profitable project. (Author interview, Founder 6)

Parent organizations often serve as learning environments for potential entrepreneurs who are earning a paycheck while they figure out their own venture. However, not all companies are expected to be fertile habitats. Lower-performing parents may spread low-performing routines that are unhelpful to entrepreneurship and need to be unlearned. Simply put, mediocrity tends to breed mediocrity.

Smaller companies are expected to provide a broader learning experience by allowing the employee greater access to the entire business operation rather than to just one unit or department with narrower responsibilities. Small companies usually have flatter hierarchies, that is, fewer levels of management. Flat organizational hierarchies allow members increased access to information and greater inclusion in the strategic functions of the business. Employees get to see what is going on in marketing, purchasing, customer service, engineering, R&D, operations, and finance. They sit at the same table for the big meetings and get to hear what is being discussed.

They are part of or at least closer to the company's strategic management processes. Smaller firms offer a training ground for entrepreneurial behaviors.[1] Their employees get involved with new initiatives because there is no one else to do it. Getting exposure to the different functions of the organization and interacting with a wide array of industry stakeholders is invaluable to future entrepreneurship.

In small companies, employees get a privileged view of the whole operation, or a good chunk of it, owing to its overall small size.

Of particular interest are our results suggesting that small firms play an important performance-related role in generating not only numerous entrepreneurs, but also particularly successful ones. This is a key result, because potential entrepreneurs, managers, and policy makers alike may make different decisions depending on whether they view the dynamics of entry into entrepreneurship as driven primarily by factors that relate directly to productivity or merely by preferences quite unrelated to performance. We find that employees working in small firms engage in becoming entrepreneurs. Moreover, we find that new entrepreneurs coming from small firms supervise more workers in their entrepreneurial start-ups and earn more in early stages of entrepreneurship than their large firm counterparts, even after controlling for ability (as measured by their previous wage) and prior activities on the job. We speculate that this may come from an increased capacity for opportunity recognition [...], greater access to networks and resources that are valuable

---

[1] R. Strohmeyer and R. Leicht. 2000. "Small Training Firms: A Breeding Ground for Self-Employment?" *International Journal of Sociology* 30, no. 4, pp. 59–89.

in entrepreneurship [...], or better self-assessment of entrepreneurial talent. (Elfenbein et al. 2010, 661)[2]

Although small organizations may make for effective training grounds, large, well-managed ones can allocate resources internally, creating an internal market for new ventures within themselves. This is advantageous and would interest someone like Rich Barton, who created Expedia within Microsoft as an internal corporate venture, which Microsoft eventually spun off, triggering Barton to leave to found spinout Zillow.[3] As a bonus, the presence of an internal market expands opportunities for employee advancement through intrapreneurship. This should make it less likely that employees are unable to find the entrepreneurial experiences they are seeking. One founder describes his experience as follows:

> [My employer] was a $500 million company—very large. These were just pet projects that were outside of their main business, you know just right place right time, I got to do far more than I would ever have gone to do in any other place. It was like running a small company. A company with 2–4 million revenue is not huge but I got to directly report to the president and CEO of a really big company. I got that mentorship. It was like running a really tiny part of the company but I reported directly to the president, that was pretty good. (Author interview, Founder 14)

When it was growing, Google wanted to keep employees who were keen to start their own companies or join a high-rocketing startup. That is one of the reasons it developed an in-house incubator allowing Google employees to develop their startups within the company.[4]

---

[2] D.W. Elfenbein, B.H. Hamilton, and T.R. Zenger. 2010. "The Small Firm Effect and the Entrepreneurial Spawning of Scientists and Engineers," *Management Science* 56, no. 4, pp. 659–681.

[3] See Zillow case.

[4] I. Kar. July 21, 2022. "Google's Plan to Make Sure Its Employees Don't Leave for Startups Is an In-House 'Start-Up Incubator,'" *Quartz.* https://qz.com/669499/googles-plan-to-make-sure-its-employees-dont-leave-for-startups-is-an-in-house-start-up-incubator

Large organizations have more resources and information and can better support internal corporate ventures.[5] Therefore, with an internal market for innovations, large firms with sufficient resources can absorb more of their potential spinouts or else spin them off later. For example, Alphabet is a well-known incubator for dozens of new ventures. Alphabet has the financial heft to do this (at the moment), but few firms are in its league.

Parent structure also may affect learning opportunities for employees. Some organizations use silos to, for example, structurally separate exploration and exploitation activities and let senior managers do the tie-backs between the two activities.[6] Some go so far as forbidding their employees from talking to each other about work unless seated in the same unit together. For instance, Apple employees going to lunch in the shared courtyard may not discuss their work with employees from other units.

Apart from its size and potential as a learning environment, the parent firm's disposition toward employee entrepreneurship matters a lot. While some may become hostile, others may adapt by partnering with spinouts.

Parent Organization Benevolence

Parent firms with positive attitudes can act as powerful enablers. We have documented different parent companies and their friendly approaches to spinouts.

AstraZeneca[7] has an explicit program that tries to spin out innovations that the organization itself cannot pursue simply because it has so many other better options to invest in first. The strategy is to seek out investors and other stakeholders to support a new company that takes the innovation and some human resources in a licensing deal with the parent. AstraZeneca has a scouting team devoted to this purpose. This approach is desirable for AstraZeneca because it allows employees' sticky

---

[5] A. Kacperczyk and M. Marx. 2016. "Revisiting the Small-Firm Effect on Entrepreneurship: Evidence From Firm Dissolutions," *Organization Science* 27, no. 4, pp. 893–910.

[6] C.A. O'Reilly III and M.L. Tushman. 2013. "Organizational Ambidexterity: Past, Present, and Future," *Academy of management Perspectives* 27, no. 4, pp. 324–338.

[7] See AstraZeneca case.

tacit knowledge to go along with the intellectual property that it gives up for a 20 percent stake in the spinout to the parent. Otherwise, they could simply try to sell or license their patents to others, which is difficult because tacit knowledge cannot be written down in a patent. AstraZeneca scouts actively pitch its spinout ideas to consortia of outside investors to make deals happen.

There has been some research examining the role of parent-spinout ownership and control relationships. Overall, the evidence seems to point toward the need for spinouts to have greater independence. Thus, AstraZeneca's 20 percent stake seems reasonable if it gives up control.

Nokia's[8] bridge program is an example of extraordinary parent benevolence as it allows employees in a downsized division to exit with one of Nokia's innovations in hand. The spinout serves as a kind of "lifeboat" for laid-off employees. After enduring a major drop in its phone sales once affordable smartphones took off in the mainstream market, Nokia needed time to put out a smartphone of its own. As it rushed to develop one, it cut back its workforce, especially those parts that were actively developing incremental innovations to its existing line of traditional mobile phones. Nokia employees were notified of their impending release and offered a unique proposition. They could continue to work on one of the parent's innovations they felt was the most promising. They could take it outside the company yet receive the parent's full support to make the venture viable through bridge funding. Interested employees went through business planning courses and developed business plans before they went out the door. This example of spinout-friendly corporate behavior shows what is possible if a parent is so inclined. Nokia-level benevolence is unheard of in North America. We interviewed a former Nokia insider to get their perspective on Nokia's bridge program.

> I would say here are the ways that it helped me: number one, it helped me incubate the idea that we had for [the spinout]. So all the work that we did at Nokia actually fit into [the spinout] from a research perspective, all the tests we ran, we learned what things work, what things didn't, it helped us to build the right thing into [the spinout], the knowledge of the domain and the product space

---

[8] See Nokia case.

that I developed in Nokia helps. Also from a practical perspective, Nokia shut down the lab and as part of that we had a program where employees could apply to take their work and spin it out as a business. So Nokia accepted my application to spin out [the spinout] as a separate business, they gave me the idea release and the grant to take the work that I was doing in Nokia and spin it out as a business. [T]here are super famous examples of companies coming out of the bridge program and being successful. As Scandinavian a company with Scandinavian values they wanted to take care of the employees that were laid off, that was part of it. I think those are the two biggest ways that it helped me. (Author interview, Founder 16)

Palantir has emerged as an affable and impactful incubator of spinouts. Their alums are dubbed the Palantir Pack because so many have started their own ventures.

In one study, researchers show that Bangladesh's giant garment industry is partly due to spinouts from the early foreign multinationals that started the industry there.[9] There are also examples of how Flipkart and Zoho both boosted India's economy through their spinouts. Flipkart, which is a spinout of Amazon, has become a prolific parent responsible for some of the fastest-growing startups in India. One source suggests there are over 150 Flipkart spinouts, which have together raised over $10 billion in capital.

This entrepreneurial tendency of Flipkart employees, or "Flipsters," has a lot to do with the company culture, regarded as highly-collaborative with an emphasis on bringing and executing individual ideas. In fact, this entrepreneurial drive is a key characteristic that the company looks for while hiring. In an interview with The Representative, Nithin Seth, former COO of Flipkart,

---

[9] R. Mostafa and S. Klepper. 2018. "Industrial Development Through Tacit Knowledge Seeding: Evidence From the Bangladesh Garment Industry," *Management Science* 64, no. 2, pp. 613–632.

shared, "When we look into the profile of a candidate—we look for people who have a very high drive for action, execution, and high customer orientation. We look for a thing that we can call 'audacity'—they think they are entrepreneurial and they are very good problem solvers." (Singh 2023, para. 5)[10]

Companies like Intel[11] are selectively friendly toward their spinouts. Its policy allows spinouts of manufacturing technologies so that Intel can prioritize the design work. However, the company is reputed to be hostile toward spinouts that have the potential to compete with them.

Spinout Networks

Spinouts fan out, but many still maintain a network of ties to their parents and to their siblings as well. This arrangement is mutually beneficial as parents may become secure anchor firms for their offspring. One scholar did a qualitative study of a prolific Israeli parent RAD, that is, in the networking components business:

> The uniqueness of RAD and its founders stems from the fact that since its establishment, a large number of startup firms have emerged from the original core of RAD [...]. The company fostered startups within its own group, and many "alumni/ae" of RAD left to form their own startups, with technologies quite different at times from those of the "mother ship." A vast ecosystem of some 100 firms exists and can be used as a case study for examining entrepreneurial spin-offs enterprises. As such, the case of RAD can serve as a microeconomics laboratory to investigate

---

[10] S. Singh. February 15, 2023. "Inside the Flipkart Mafia—Five Companies Founded by Former Employees of India's Biggest Tech Startup," *THE ORG.* https://theorg.com/iterate/inside-the-flipkart-mafia-five-companies-founded-by-former-employees-of

[11] See the Intel case.

the policy implications of innovation driven by the "mother ship" process. (Frenkel et al. 2015, 1647)[12]

In a network formation, the parent company is not necessarily the center hub, but one of many different types of stakeholders in an ecosystem of interconnected organizations. Spinouts help grow economies by contributing to regional diversification. Scholars have also demonstrated that spinouts improve the locally available labor pool. Through trial and error, people quit their jobs and later become assets to others through new employment or venturing. Even failed startups add value overall as their resources are redistributed to the highest bidder.

The researchers examining RAD concluded that: "'viral clouds' of startups like the one we studied can thus intentionally be designed and developed." Although, in reality, most networks have dominant and subordinate players, there is great potential for innovation to spread out in many different directions.

This view increases the probability of spinout-to-spinout transactions. For example, Zoho is an Indian startup that sells office tools online. It has 10,000 employees. Zoho has been credited with indirectly creating another 8,000 jobs through the hiring done by its 22 spinouts. Worthwhile interactions can occur between and among spinouts of the same parent. One author describes the interactivity between some Zoho spinouts as follows: "Freshworks uses Chargebee for subscription management, Facilio uses Freshchat for website conversation, Hippo video use Freshdesk for customer support" (Da 2019).[13]

Enabling Institutions

The institutional setting can enable spinouts. Let's discuss competition-friendly jurisdictions, benefits programs, and open innovation strategies.

---

[12] A. Frenkel, E. Israel, and S. Maital. 2015. "The Evolution of Innovation Networks and Spin-Off Entrepreneurship: The Case of RAD," *European Planning Studies* 23, no. 8, pp. 1646–1670.

[13] N. Da. March 1, 2019. "Zoho Mafia: 22 Companies Founded by Former Zoho Employees," *HackerNoon*. https://hackernoon.com/zoho-mafia-16-companies-founded-by-former-zoho-employees-eafac85ff2ea

Competition-Friendly Jurisdictions

Since California's ban on noncompetes has long been associated with a vibrant startup culture, other jurisdictions are taking note. An enabling trend that is slowly but steadily gaining traction is to weaken or ban non-compete clauses embedded in employment contracts. Since it is widely believed to be in the public interest to have more competition among companies, not less, most restrictive covenants that reduce competition are difficult to justify.[14]

As a recent example of changes to institutions that enable entrepreneurship in Canada, the province of Ontario has enacted legislation that includes a ban on noncompete clauses in employment contracts. As its justification, the province said it did not want free trade to be impeded by such agreements. "Effective October 25, 2021 employers are prohibited from entering into employment contracts or other agreements with an employee that include a non-compete agreement."[15] Whether this law will have a significant effect on new venture formation depends largely on the enforceability of other types of restrictive covenants, like nonsolicitations and nondisclosures.

Hawaii recently banned noncompetes for technology workers. But Hawaii's targeting of high-tech workers in particular is insightful. The islands' potential as a hub for remote workers and tech organizations that can be located anywhere globally is palpable. The objective is to encourage more of the high-tech diaspora to make the islands their home, thereby growing the tax base and helping to build the economy. Interestingly, the state chose not to ban noncompetes in all the lower-tech industries. Apparently, policy makers believe it would not be desirable to have more competition in those traditional industries.

Conversely, some European countries do ban noncompetes for "blue collar" workers, arguing that it cannot be in the public interest to limit

---

[14] S. Samila and O. Sorenson. 2011. "Noncompete Covenants: Incentives to Innovate or Impediments to Growth," *Management Science* 57, no. 3, pp. 425–438.

[15] Ontario.ca. 2023. "Non-Compete Agreements | Your Guide to the Employment Standards Act." www.ontario.ca/document/your-guide-employment-standards-act-0/non-compete-agreements (accessed March 15, 2023).

new companies created by such employees. In many countries, even for managers or executives to be restrained by an enforceable noncompete, the parent firm must continue to pay them some portion of their salary after their employment ends. In many European countries, parent organizations must often pay 50 to 100 percent of the leaver's salary for the duration of the restriction period. Moreover, restrictions are often limited to three or six months instead of years, as permitted in the strictest U.S. states like Florida. These examples of public policy from Europe recognize the value inherent in employee mobility and employee entrepreneurship. There appears to be heightened political recognition that fostering entrepreneurial ecosystems with many startups is preferable to higher risk reliance on a few large companies. America's Rust Belt is a case in point.

Benefits Programs

Health care insurance benefits and pensions that are tied to a particular employer may present a two-edged sword. The sharper side cuts job insecurity, helping to retain workers. The other is a dull blade holding back potential leavers who worry about losing their employment benefits, be they founders or acolytes that might join the spinout team. By contrast, when the benefits and pension system is separate from the employer, typically provided by government-funded health care and tax-sheltered individual retirement accounts, there are fewer worries about leaving a regular paycheck and trying something new. Similarly, in countries with socialized medicine, access to medical care is not tied to a particular employer, so employees do not lose this important security if they venture out on their own.

Open Innovation Strategies

How can parent organizations share intellectual property rights with their employees in a mutually beneficial way? Is it possible to minimize or eliminate friction over intellectual property to allow spinouts while protecting the parent's best interests? Yes, there may be a way.

Combining a spinout-friendly parent firm with enabling institutions yields the concept of open innovation. Open innovation challenges the notion of strict intellectual property rights by blurring the lines between ownership and use.

Open innovation is understanding that many innovations are going to come from outside and not from inside the company. It involves exploiting to best advantage innovations from outside the firm while sharing some of the firm's innovations with the community at large.[16] This reciprocity ensures the firm gets access to the latest developments in technology but also gives back by posting modifications and improvements to a central repository. As a side benefit, it greatly reduces an industry's administrative and legal costs to bring and defend against lawsuits alleging IP theft.

Open innovation is a movement, philosophy, and strategy rooted in the belief that sharing technology and information is more practicable than hoarding it. For example, when software developers post their code on websites like GitHub, others can freely use that code for their own purposes. The posting developer receives wider recognition for writing good code, which may lead to a promotion, other job opportunities, or invitations to join a spinout. A Creative Commons license is typically used to manage the intellectual property in open-source repositories. Rules governing use of IP might stipulate that a licensee must reciprocate by posting any improvements they make to the code. Other rules would require acknowledging whose IP was used and perhaps some restrictions for certain types of commercial use without express permission. A case example follows.

Zoom is a spinout of Cisco, and the founder persuaded some 40 engineers to join the new company. Though California law does not allow noncompetes, it does permit other types of restrictive covenants, especially affecting intellectual property rights in nondisclosure agreements and patents. Many of the components that Zoom engineers needed for

---

[16] H. Chesbrough. 2012. "Open Innovation: Where We've Been and Where We're Going," *Research-Technology Management* 55, no. 4, pp. 20–27.

its software were available in open-source repositories, avoiding any friction with Cisco. Many IP holders object to their code being posted on open repositories and may forbid it. However, other employers are realizing that the need to attract and retain high-quality, innovative employees should outweigh their fears about open sourcing.

While open innovation is often thought of as a process for existing organizations to gain access to outside sources of innovation, it can also help startups, so long as the ground rules are equitable for both parties, giving each a decent shot at reaching their potential.

New thinking about coordination between parent organizations and spinouts is emerging from the "open strategy" literature. The basic premise is to stop hiding the company's business strategy. Instead, make the strategy transparent to stakeholders, who can decide whether to participate based on their perceived role in the company's strategy.

Case Study: The Palantir Pack

Founded in 2003, Palantir is a business-to-business (B2B) information technology services company whose customers are large corporate and government organizations looking to solve big problems in their industries.

Palantir's parent firm was PayPal, and they share a history of mentorship and seed investment from controversial billionaire Peter Theil, whose experience with credit card fraud at PayPal served as a motivation to start Palantir.[17] Theil invested $40 million at the start and recruited Lonsdale, the company's first CEO after he had interned at PayPal while still a student at Stanford.

Corporate Culture

Lonsdale was a continuous innovator who promoted a culture that allowed the entrepreneurial spirit of employees to thrive, whether internally or

---

[17] A. Hartmans. March 19, 2021. "Nearly a Dozen Major Tech Firms Can Trace Their Roots to PayPal. From Palantir to Tesla, Here Are the Companies Launched by Members of the 'PayPal Mafia,'" *Business Insider*. www.businessinsider.com/tech-companies-founded-by-paypal-mafia-full-list-2020-10

externally. An early employee describes his attraction to the company's values: "It was quite evident that Palantir had a wonderful vision and concentration, and was incredibly aggressive in its approach toward innovation and a lot of fundamentally broken things."[18]

More than 170 companies were created by former Palantir executives and employees,[19] a whole ecosystem of related businesses with potential opportunities for Palantir, its mobile employees, and entrepreneurial founders.

Corporate Strategy and Spinouts

Palantir is a rare corporate shape-shifter. As the business moves and shifts from one industry to the next, it generates spinouts in those new areas, too. For example, when Palantir concentrated its services on the health sector, it began to sprout more spinouts in that industry.

Little Otter is a pediatric mental health solution provider founded by Palantir alum, suggesting that the parent firm's spinout strategy is transferable to different industries.

Palantir spinouts typically do not build on the parent's products. They use different technologies, next-generation technologies, and tackle different problems. Palantir does not invest in its spinouts, but some of its investors do.

True to form, Lonsdale left Palantir in 2009 and built a venture fund called Formation 8 that invests primarily in Palantir alumni. He also founded OpenGov.com, which provides business IT services to cities.

Outcomes

Palantir continues to produce new founders at a good clip. But unlike PayPal, there is no exodus happening all in one shot due to an external shock like an acquisition. For example, alums account for four of the

---

[18] "The Startup That's Spawning a New Generation of Startups." n.d. www.inc .com/jeremy-quittner/palantir-and-the-spinoff-effect.html

[19] B. Carson. August 27, 2022. "Silicon Valley's Newest Mafia: The Palantir Pack," *Protocol.* www.protocol.com/palantir-pack-alumni-startups

summer 2022 Y Combinator batch: Ilumadata, Moonshot, Medplum, and Windmill.[20]

According to Crunchbase,[21] 101 startups are registered in its database with Palantir as a parent organization, including 248 founders, with 20 percent being acquired and 3 percent going public with an IPO. One of the most successful startups from Palantir alums is RelateIQ (big data for CRM), founded by two former Palantir employees, which was bought by Salesforce in 2013 for U.S. $400 million.

Implications

- Parent firms can provide learning environments that encourage spinouts.
- Alumni networks are valuable means of acquiring resources for spinouts.
- Spinouts can boost a parent firm's reputation as an innovative place to work.

Case Study: Nokia's Benevolence in a Downturn

Nokia offers a unique parent firm story. The large phone maker was in trouble in 2012 when its products became uncompetitive due to the introduction of smartphones by Apple and Samsung. To mitigate the impact of layoffs, Nokia encouraged employees to do spinouts as a bridge into entrepreneurship.

Parent Firm Background

The company was established in 1865 by mining engineer Fredrik Idestam as a paper mill operation in Tampere, Finland. Nokia got its name from the location of a second mill, which was built along the Nokianvirta

---

[20] "Silicon Valley's Newest Mafia: The Palantir Pack." August 27, 2022. *Protocol.* www.protocol.com/palantir-pack-alumni-startups

[21] www.crunchbase.com/hub/palantir-technologies-alumni-founded-companies

river.[22] It pioneered and was successful in various manufacturing sectors, including paper products, rubber boots, tires, cable, televisions, and mobile phones.[23] It introduced the first camera phone in 2003, enjoying seven years of increasing sales, and became the world leader.

Downturn

New competitors with smartphones made Nokia's handsets less attractive to customers and led to a steep decline in revenues and stock prices. By 2011, Nokia established a strategic alliance with Microsoft in an attempt to stay competitive. However, Nokia was in deep trouble and, a year later, had to close many of its businesses.[24] The company's restructuring led to 18,000 layoffs across 13 countries. This resulted in significant hardship for affected employees, their families, and communities. Nokia sold its mobile and devices division to Microsoft in 2014.[25]

The Bridge Program

Even though Nokia was unable to prevent the layoffs, its executives tried to provide employees with a softer landing. The bridge program allowed employees to pursue a new business idea by leveraging their skills and accomplishments from Nokia as well as the parent firm's associated intellectual property to build their startup. As a result of the program, most of the employees had developed a business plan and were ready to start their venture the day they left the company. The bridge program assisted employees in launching over 1,000 new businesses in the communities

---

[22] A. Potoroaca. November 24, 2022. "Nokia: The Story of the Once-Legendary Phone Maker," *TechSpot*. www.techspot.com/article/2236-nokia/

[23] Nokia. 2023. "Our History | Nokia." www.nokia.com/about-us/company/our-history/ (accessed March 15, 2023).

[24] "The Impact of an Entrepreneur's Knowledge—A Case of Nokia's Spinoff." n.d. www.diva-portal.org/smash/get/diva2:1179970/FULLTEXT01.pdf

[25] Nokia. 2023. "Our History | Nokia." www.nokia.com/about-us/company/our-history/ (accessed March 15, 2023).

where Nokia was a significant industry employer.[26] For example, Oulu-talent is a team of 500 ex-Nokia employees based in the Finnish town of Oulu. The company has generated more than 50 devices.[27]

The bridge program also had some positive effects on Nokia. First, it helped Nokia to create an ecosystem of startups around itself, which can be helpful for knowledge sharing in the future.[28] Half of Nokia spinouts had ongoing technology licensing deals with the parent, each bringing in revenue.[29] Second, Nokia earned a favorable reputation among stakeholders who viewed it as a model of a benevolent parent firm.

Implications

- Parent firms can enable spinouts through IP sharing and training.
- Spinouts can be lifeboats for employees when corporations downsize.
- Spinouts can reduce the blow of layoffs on communities.

---

[26] "Harvard Business Publishing Education." 2023. https://hbsp.harvard.edu/product/315003-PDF-ENG (accessed March 15, 2023).

[27] "TechCrunch Is Part of the Yahoo Family of Brands." July 24, 2012. https://techcrunch.com/2012/07/24/as-nokia-completes-scalado-purchase-another-ambitious-ex-employee-spinoff-emerges-oulutalent/

[28] S. Sucher. 2023. "There's a Better Way to Do Layoffs: What Nokia Learned, the Hard Way." www.linkedin.com/pulse/theres-better-way-do-layoffs-what-nokia-learned-hard-sandra-sucher (accessed March 15, 2023).

[29] B. Kang, H. Rannikko, and E.T. Tornikoski. December 1, 2017. "How a Laid-Off Employee Becomes an Entrepreneur: The Case of Nokia's Bridge Program." *Ideas.Repec.Org.* https://ideas.repec.org/p/hit/iirwps/17-15.html

CHAPTER 6

Benefits and Challenges for Parent Organizations

Relatively few parent companies are as spinout friendly as Palantir and AstraZeneca, but there are four main reasons why it would be in their best interests to be so. They are corporate coherence, knowledge spillbacks, attractive acquisition targets, and reputation for incubation.

Robust arguments based on evidence showing net positives for parent organizations may help when negotiating more flexible employment contracts, shareholder agreements, and, of course, exit conditions. Job seekers may also want to assess whether a potential employer stays abreast of modern management techniques. Does this company have a mature, progressive spinout policy and procedure? If it does, the door is likely open to a mutual symbiotic relationship.

Corporate Coherence

Consider, for example, William Durant, who left GM's Buick division over conflicts with the company's broader acquisition strategy [...] He set up Chevrolet to pursue the production of a smaller car that he had championed and developed while at Buick, aiming to compete with Ford's Model T. Chevrolet was set up in Flint, Michigan, and it successfully produced and commercialized Durant's smaller car. In fact, by 1915, the car was ranked 10th in industry sales, and subsequent performance was even more impressive. Meanwhile, although Buick had completely abandoned Durant's project of producing this smaller car, during the same period, its sales of relatively larger cars actually increased from about 43,946 cars in 1914 to 255,160 by 1927 [...]. Usually, when founders or top executives disagreed and decided to exit to entrepreneurship, they would also take their project with them, as Durant did. Thus, in most cases the parent organization would drop the project all together, as GM did, and would focus on its core project instead (Ioannou 2014, 536).[1]

In this case, the innovation did not fit GM's business model, so the visionary was not given the time of day, let alone any corporate investment in smaller cars. Large car sales were on the upswing; understandably, GM continued manufacturing the vehicles they knew best and had established a profitable market for. Company executives usually do not stick their necks out for innovations that do not look any better than the current business or improve the current business. Therefore, so long as the innovation remains under parental control, it is not going anywhere. But why not let it go? It could have a bright future as a spinout and simultaneously strengthen the parent's corporate coherence.

A strong strategy-based argument is that organizations thrive best on coherence; they should ideally contain a set of businesses and business activities that are in good alignment with each other and not pull in too many different directions. In particular, there should be synergies between the businesses, such as sharing the same marketing, IT department, distribution, or manufacturing.

Most companies have finite resources and cannot take on all the innovations they create. But if they did, the result would be significant incoherence. Undisciplined and unfocused spending on innovation leaves too many balls to juggle, especially for a centralized business that relies on a small number of top managers for strategic decisions. Andy Grove (former leader of Intel) described most innovations in chip technology as "distractions" unworthy of investigation because they could never equal the size and profitability of the current microprocessor business.

New ideas, in a company that is already growing its core business, are often viewed as annoying distractions. So why not allow employees

---

[1] I. Ioannou. 2014. "When Do Spinouts Enhance Parent Firm Performance? Evidence From the US Automobile Industry, 1890–1986," *Organization Science* 25, no. 2, pp. 529–551.

to exploit peripheral ideas outside the company? For example, when Intel approved the spinouts of manufacturing technologies related to chip-making, it freed itself to put all its energy into design. Such singular attention may help the leader in a fast-improving technology sector to stay ahead of the pack.

Strategic alignment has long been an important theme in strategy research, management literature, and teaching. Managers are advised to align the organization to support and grow the core business and out-source the rest. There are three relevant levels of strategy: functional, business, and corporate.[2] Corporate coherence indicates there is strategic alignment, for instance, among functional area strategies and business level strategies.

At the business level, an emphasis on low cost, differentiation, and broad or narrow customer segments can lead to incoherence. For exam-ple, when a company specializing in low-cost products develops an internal corporate venture selling to luxury customers, it may confuse customers and make it more difficult for internal stakeholders and man-agers to decide what is most important and what overall direction the organization is moving in.

At the corporate level, strategy research suggests that only related diversification is valuable, whereas unrelated diversification should be avoided. Shedding unaligned business units, even at the early stages, can better align the company around one cohesive strategy. Unrelated diver-sification leading to conglomerates is detrimental to organizational per-formance, for instance, GE under Jack Welch acquired a media company, an investment bank, and other unrelated businesses.[3] Welch perhaps immodestly declared that the core capability of GE was its management style. GE has now shed most of these noncore holdings and just recently announced it was doing a "final" splitoff into three separate "pure play"

---

[2] C.W. Hill, G.R. Jones and M.A. Schilling. 2014. "Strategic Management: Theory and Cases: An Integrated Approach," *Cengage Learning*.

[3] "How Jack Welch Destroyed Sloan's Century | GPI." 2023. https://globalpi.org/research/how-jack-welch-destroyed-sloans-century/ (accessed March 15, 2023).

companies (aviation, power, and medical).[4] Today's investors express their disapproval of overly diversified companies with a diversification discount. A discounted stock price puts pressure on corporate leaders to sell off unrelated business ventures that develop internally, lest they become takeover targets by opportunists with deeper pockets. This discount is largely explained by the incompetence of central managers, who sometimes try to force synergies where they do not work well together. Imagine the marketing department that has to navigate both customer and business-to-business. Or consider the R&D department that is shared across 10 different industries.

Conglomerates fail because they spend too much or too little on "distractions" due to their limited decision-making capacities and insufficient information. This is the predictable outcome of centralized decision making in excessively diversified firms. If noncore businesses were instead funded by external investors, the pattern might be very different[5] and perhaps more optimal.

In sum, for many parents, hanging onto unaligned businesses is worse than letting them go! Andy Grove suggested that, while an organization might have hundreds of innovative internal projects on the go, only those candidates with enough potential to eclipse the current core business would be important enough to bank on. All other projects are distractions that should be jettisoned or, at best, kept alive at low activity levels to retain a strategic footprint.

Knowledge Spillbacks

Over time, a spinout's usable knowledge can flow back to the parent. The maintenance of social ties between former colleagues allows for a

---

[4] J. Cornell. December 14, 2021. "General Electric Announces Plan to Separate into Three Independent Publicly Traded Companies," *Forbes*. www.forbes.com/sites/joecornell/2021/12/14/general-electric-announces-plan-to-separate-into-three-independent-publicly-traded-companies/

[5] D. Hoechle, M. Schmid, I. Walter, and D. Yermack. 2012. "How Much of the Diversification Discount Can Be Explained by Poor Corporate Governance?" *Journal of Financial Economics* 103, no. 1, pp. 41–60.

flow of knowledge back and forth.[6] Knowledge spillbacks from spinouts ("entrants") may produce a virtuous cycle whereby both the parent and the spinouts benefit from each other's innovations.

> [T]he process of creative destruction is but one end of the continuum; with the other end representing a process of creative construction—a process wherein entrants benefit from new knowledge created by incumbent organizations that may otherwise be left unexploited, but where such knowledge spillovers do not necessarily result in the destruction of incumbents. As entrants build on knowledge and networks developed by incumbent organizations to create new novel combinations that in a Schumpeterian sense causes the destruction of lesser entities, reverse flows from entrants to incumbents can lead to a dynamic process of growth, and thereby a win-win scenario where the positive externalities of knowledge spillovers are highlighted in the process of both value creation and appropriation (Agarwal et al. 2007, 264).[7]

Optimally, knowledge transfer goes both ways. The parent has an opportunity to learn from the innovations of their spinouts and may view them as potential strategic footholds. The rise of spinouts is said to be evidence in favor of the creative construction theory of entrepreneurship.[8] This theory holds the spinout as a positive phenomenon for parent firms because of the potential for knowledge transfers. It is the opposite of Schumpeter's "creative destruction" theory, where the spinout is a potentially disruptive competitor.

---

[6] J.Y. Kim and H.K. Steensma. 2017. "Employee Mobility, Spin-Outs, and Knowledge Spill-In: How Incumbent Firms Can Learn From New Ventures," *Strategic Management Journal* 38, no. 8 pp. 1626– 1645.

[7] R. Agarwal, D. Audretsch, and M.B. Sarkar. 2007. "The Process of Creative Construction: Knowledge Spillovers, Entrepreneurship, and Economic Growth," *Strategic Entrepreneurship Journal* 1, no. 3–4, pp. 263–286.

[8] J.Y. Kim and H.K. Steensma. 2017. "Employee Mobility, Spin-outs, and Knowledge Spill-In: How Incumbent Firms Can Learn From New Ventures," *Strategic Management Journal* 38, no. 8, pp. 1626–1645.

From a networked organization perspective, we can view a parent organization as part of a web of social ties with people working within both the parent and its spinouts. Scholars have noted the ease of employee mobility across such networks. It is easier for a parent to learn from its spinouts because of the social ties that already exist between the organizations that facilitate knowledge transfer in both directions. Thus, both the spinout and the parent can benefit from knowledge spillbacks.

There is a tendency for mobility of employees to and from the spinout, and to and from the parent. The two-way flow allows for human capital to be the main mechanism of transmission between them. Imagine if a parent has 10 spinouts, there is so much more to learn than from only one, although peer relations can also occur. Spinouts often advance innovations that are relevant to the parent organization because of their inheritance.

The knowledge also transfers more smoothly back to the parent because the spinout tends to share many of the same routines as the parent; they may use similar language to communicate, and they may have similar belief systems about some things. There is evidence that spinouts tend to inherit strategies, tactics, and routines from their parent organization, including human resource strategies, equity and inclusion approaches, and marketing tactics.

Organizations have been called fountains (or fonts) of partially firm-specific knowledge and skills, beliefs and values, social capital, and opportunities.[9] In the analogy, employees drink from the fountain and get to know the taste of the water and get used to it. This results in a lower degree of effort to communicate between parent and spinout. They are more likely to share some of the same tastes. Shared routines quicken knowledge transfers not only when the employees depart to pursue their ventures but also afterwards, as they continue to benefit from the relationship. The inherent synergy between parent and spinout enables a long-term relationship of knowledge sharing. This can include sharing market or technical information through conversations, presentations, publications, or patents.

---

[9] J.B. Sørensen and M.A. Fassiotto. 2011. "Organizations as Fonts of Entrepreneurship," *Organization Science* 22, no. 5, pp. 1322–1331.

Spinouts Make Attractive Acquisition Targets

One can only imagine the scale of knowledge spillovers out of Cisco Systems in its heyday. It was the main backbone of the Internet, valued in the hundreds of billions of dollars. After its hugely successful IPO, swimming in cash also meant lots of room for R&D and internal corporate ventures. The company produced a great number of innovations, but it could not pursue them all with equal vigor. For instance, Zoom is a product of Cisco's resource allocation process.

In fact, having incubated so many spinouts and with so much capital at its disposal, Cisco had the luxury of selecting from among the best for reacquisition. They used the term spin-ins to describe an acquisition of a company's own spinouts.[10] Cisco's top managers acknowledged that talent and ideas freely walked out the door, so often, the best course of action was to buy some of them back and reintegrate into the parent. Cisco was effectively using its spinouts as strategic beachheads to keep an eye on new innovations that could be brought back into the fold. It works because Cisco naturally knows more about its own spinouts than any other potential acquirer. One group of former Cisco employees have reportedly sold four startups to Cisco,[11] suggesting spinouts were so common that they were a matter of routine.

As more evidence emerges from studies of corporate data, we learn that many mergers and acquisitions face difficulties integrating new technologies. Acquirers often pay too much and overestimate the synergies they can get from merger activities.

Getting acquired is often a lucrative way for entrepreneurs to cash out of a business. Some startups seem to be purpose-built to be bought out. There is no genuine attempt to build a company, only a facade that looks impressive in a presentation and can be acquired quite painlessly, or so it appears. For startup founders, acquisition can result in a windfall as their

[10] R.A. Hunt, D.M. Townsend, E. Asgari, and D.A. Lerner. 2019. "Bringing It All Back Home: Corporate Venturing and Renewal Through Spin-Ins," *Entrepreneurship Theory and Practice* 43, no.6, pp. 1166–1193.

[11] "Yahoo Is Part of the Yahoo Family of Brands." 2023. https://ca.news.yahoo .com/ex-cisco-engineers-raise-278-213426935.html (accessed March 15, 2023).

shares are absorbed by the acquiring organization or potentially move on to other things.

Acquisitions are often not successful and can have unanticipated consequences. For example, when eBay bought PayPal,[12] it did not anticipate the exodus of its core executive and development team due to organizational cultural incompatibilities. eBay tried to impose its performance measurement culture on PayPal, while the latter preferred an innovation-driven approach that did not count the pennies.

Research suggests that acquisitions of spinouts by their own parent firms are more likely and more successful because the odds are better for a good fit.[13] The parent is also more likely to have access to information about the spinout's prospects because of their continuing social relations, that is, less information asymmetry between the two. Such a spinout also makes for a smoother acquisition thanks to inherited routines that make reintegration and coordination easier.

From the perspective of the buyer, preferential information about the spinout's prospects allows an offer price that better matches actual potential rather than overpaying. This helps to alleviate one of the biggest problems that companies face when trying to buy from other companies, which is the uncertainty and ambiguity of facts about opportunities. Information asymmetry refers to the differences in the information available to buyers and sellers. When there is less information asymmetry, more confident and competent buying decisions can be made. It helps managers to develop plans for what parts of the acquired business could be merged or assimilated and which parts will be preserved and invested in. More thorough knowledge means smarter pricing.

One of the biggest challenges that acquisitions face is the integration phase. Often mergers fail because of persistent differences in organizational culture or because of incompatible routines. Again, spinouts often share more commonalities with the parent, so when a parent acquires its spinouts, it can probably also integrate them effectively.

---

[12] See Paypal case.

[13] R.A. Hunt, D.M. Townsend, E. Asgari, and D.A. Lerner. 2019. "Bringing It All Back Home: Corporate Venturing and Renewal Through Spin-Ins," *Entrepreneurship Theory and Practice* 43, no. 6, pp. 1166–1193.

In a reversal of expected roles, spinouts may also become exit opportunities for parent firms. As seen in the Fairchild case, the spinouts can sometimes become more successful than the parent. Fairchild was eventually out-competed by its own offspring and was then bought and tossed around. But sometimes, it is the spinout that gobbles up the parent. A good example is Howard Schultz, who left his directorship at Starbucks to form his coffee startup, which became successful enough to make it possible for him to acquire Starbucks. He liked the brand better than his own and proceeded to use it in place of his Il Giornale brand.[14]

Reputation for Incubation

A company's reputation for incubation allows it to attract capable employees who are keen to work for a company that spawns high-quality new ventures. Research shows that spinouts boost parents' technological performance through a positive reputation as incubators, which helps them attract and retain stakeholders.[15] When a parent firm generates successful spinouts, it signals to the labor market that it's a great place for innovative and entrepreneurial employees to get a start.

For example, Palantir is known as a great place to work to develop entrepreneurial skills, allowing them to attract top technical and managerial talent. Many members of the so-called Palantir Pack have gone on to be founders. Palantir has 170 alumni who founded or led new startups after leaving the company.[16] The parent crows about these successes because they know it enhances their reputation and helps them to attract superior resources to their own endeavors, too. They even have their own syndicate with over 170 investors ready to fund the next generation of Palantir alumni startups. Management consulting firm McKinsey is

[14] D. Mendez. April 26, 2022. "The History of: Starbucks." https://scribe.usc.edu/the-history-of-starbucks/.

[15] D.G. McKendrick, J.B. Wade, and J. Jaffee. 2009. "A Good Riddance? Spin-Offs and the Technological Performance of Parent Firms," *Organization Science* 20, no. 6, pp. 979–992.

[16] B. Carson. August 27, 2022. "Silicon Valley's Newest Mafia: The Palantir Pack," *Protocol*. www.protocol.com/palantir-pack-alumni-startups

another parent that boasts about its spinouts. Its alumni have raised over $55 billion and include 15 unicorns spread across the globe.[17]

HR Software maker Lattice provides an interesting example of a parent with a venture fund to back leavers. They will fund any alum's startup to the tune of $100K, provided they do not compete with Lattice or engage in illegal activities. Other conditions are that the employee has a minimum three-year tenure at Lattice, leaves on good terms, and begins the startup within 12 months of leaving. Their CEO, Altman, claims that by investing in former employees, he can more easily filter for founders that he knows and can trust. Since Lattice invests in the startups from its own accounts, it means that every Lattice investor also gains exposure to the spinouts.

Even in organizations with no official policies, skunkworks, that is, autonomous strategic processes, are often at play. For example, former Intel CEO Andy Grove spoke of middle managers diverting resources to pet projects without the full knowledge and approval of senior managers. He was aware of some of these but allowed them to carry on as long as there was still ambiguity about the potential value of the innovations.[18] These bottom-up strategic initiatives even saved the company, materially replacing core business revenues even before being officially sanctioned by management as a central function.

In one organization we studied, Alpha (alias), generating new businesses within the firm was a principal attraction and retention mechanism. Employees often believe that variety is the spice of life. For instance, software developers do not want to spend their lives fixing legacy code issues. They want to build new things and be at the cutting edge. How does a manufacturing company keep a team of 30-plus software developers eagerly engaged? Making controllers for construction equipment is less glamorous than being at the vanguard of next-generation industrial, scientific, or military drones.

---

[17] McKinsey & Company. August 19, 2021. "Fifteen Unicorns Founded by McKinsey Alums May Be Shaping Your World." www.mckinsey.com/about-us/new-at-mckinsey-blog/fifteen-alum-founded-unicorns-that-may-have-already-changed-your-life

[18] R.A. Burgelman and A.S. Grove. 2007. "Let Chaos Reign, Then Rein in Chaos—Repeatedly: Managing Strategic Dynamics for Corporate Longevity," *Strategic Management Journal* 28, no. 10, pp. 965–979.

Alpha would purposely take contracts with outside customers, using a form of corporate venturing called "out-streaming" to help expand opportunity around the internal ventures by making them quasi-independent units. This assists Alpha to recruit and retain first-rate employees who thrive in an inventive learning environment.

In another example, one of Blackbird's creative employees wanted to go out on his own, so the management made him into a contractor. He was so good they thought they might lose him anyway. By becoming a contractor, he could offer his services to other clients and eventually grow his own firm.[19] Soon, other employees wanted the same deal too, but the bet paid off. The new culture had the effect of giving Blackbird a positive reputation as an employer that really wants its employees to be successful, even if it means letting them go. This reputation helped them to recruit from a wider pool of applicants.

Keeping Them in

Firms use many different methods to prevent unwanted spinouts or keep employees from leaving. A spinout may be unwanted because it directly challenges the perceived competitive advantage of the parent. Spinouts that take teams with them that are often led by a former manager or leader can create the most pain for parents.

We have seen that parents use restrictive covenants in employment contracts to try to reign in spinouts. However, these contracts are usually only enforced if they are narrow and fair; they also expire. A better approach might be to develop a reputation for fairness (e.g., procedural, distributive, and justice) so that employees are more likely to share their ideas with the parent. When employees trust their employers, they are more likely to stay.[20]

Employers also use compensation packages and stock ownership programs with vesting periods to keep employees from leaving. Alternatively,

---

[19] R. Bohra and J. Bhatnagar. 2022. "Case Study One Employee Went Freelance. Now Everyone Wants the Same Deal," *Harvard Business Review*. https://hbr.org/2022/03/case-study-one-employeewent-freelance-now-everyone-wants-the-same-deal

[20] J. Zábojník. 2020. "Firm Reputation, Innovation and Employee Startups," *The Economic Journal* 130, no. 627, pp. 822–851.

source firms can make sure that they commercialize employee innovations by licensing them out to others or developing internal corporate ventures. This assures employers are taking employee ideas seriously and provides a way for careers to develop internally. Nonetheless, for many firms, spinouts remain a fact of life.

Case Study: AstraZeneca

Many spinouts originate as internal corporate ventures of parent firms. However, few parents have the wherewithal to pursue all the innovations that arise from creative activities inside and outside the firm. How can management exploit these innovations in a way that is sustainable for the spinout and parent?

Parent Firm Background

AstraZeneca is among the world's largest pharmaceutical companies and recognizes the importance of knowledge sharing in the development of drug innovations. So AstraZeneca acts strategically as an incubator in the belief that it will learn from the experience of others allowed into its territory. Sometimes, these collaborations lead to a new product line or research stream.

> Delivering on our value of "We are entrepreneurial" and our strategic ambition to be a great place to work, the BioVentureHub [BVH] is stimulating a more dynamic scientific research environment at the AstraZeneca Gothenburg site.[21]

BioVentureHub is an incubator where life sciences startups develop their ventures. In 2018, it housed 26 mid-stage ventures and one academic group. Incubated startups can access to: "All technical services and general facilities, for example restaurant, meeting rooms. BVH companies can operate under AstraZeneca's environmental permit.

---

[21] Project Report. 2018. *AstraZeneca BioVentureHub*. www.azbioventurehub .com/content/dam/bioventurehub/pdf/2019/bvh_annual_report_2018.pdf

BVH company employees can also access AstraZeneca's sports centre if they have bought a membership card."[22] AstraZeneca also invests in scientific collaborations with many of the ventures, earning a reputation as a great place to innovate with access to the latest scientific ideas in a stable physical environment. "We need to continue to facilitate interaction between people, companies and organisations that do not normally interact and encourage them to work together and dare to share," said Pernilla Isberg, COO.

Even a giant has its limits in digesting all of its internal innovations. Among their own internal corporate ventures some lack the right fit for the strategic aspirations of the AstraZeneca's executive leadership. Management handpicks internal corporate ventures that make good spinout candidates and works them through a developmental process to make them a reality. The people and technology needed to make it work are allowed to flow to the spinout unimpeded. The parent retains a 20 percent stake in the spinout in exchange for cooperation on knowledge transfers.[23]

Managed Spinouts

An AstraZeneca manager contacts external investors to pitch to them an internal corporate venture as a spinout. If they get buy-in, a share of equity is negotiated in exchange for the company's resources in the form of employees, founders, intellectual property, and even facilities.

Outcomes

AstraZeneca's spinout scheme has brought mixed results, often proving difficult in practice to overcome information asymmetries and bring on external investors. But one of their big winners is OnDosis a dosage management startup.

---

[22] Ibid.

[23] W.B. Remneland and A. Styhre. 2019. "Managerial Challenges of Outbound Open Innovation: A Study of a Spinout Initiative in AstraZeneca," *R&D Management* 49, no. 4, pp. 652–667.

Implications

- Parents may want to actively push spinouts to improve their corporate coherence.
- Managers face challenges in convincing outside stakeholders of the value of innovations.
- A small, noncontrolling stake in a spinout may provide a strategic foothold.

Case Study: Fairchild

Fairchild makes for an interesting parent firm story. If you visit the Computer History Museum in Palo Alto, California, there is a long wall featuring the gamut of early microprocessor technologies. Displayed are the actual chips and technological relics with descriptions of their features, challenges, and inventors from the start of the microprocessor-driven revolution in computing that makes running software possible. There is also a graphic showing the genealogy of Silicon Valley firms based on the source of their technologies. The chip firms that fueled the valley's software companies all came from the same parent firm.

The Birth of Fairchild Semiconductor

The story begins in 1955 with William Shockley, who invented the layered transistor in his lab at Shockley Semiconductor Laboratory. He was a brilliant designer and engineer but a lousy manager, depicted as "autocratic, domineering, erratic, hard-to-please, and increasingly paranoid."[24]

When Shockley took a pass on short-term opportunities to sell silicon microprocessors, instead of championing a longer-term opportunity to

---

[24] Wikipedia Contributors. April 14, 2023. "William Shockley," *Wikipedia*. https://en.wikipedia.org/wiki/William_Shockley#cite_note-NetValley-44

develop technology for the telecom industry,[25] a group of eight engineers left to start their spinout. This was Silicon Valley's inaugural spinout and became one of the most important parent firm stories in the process. This group was subsequently labeled "The Traitorous Eight."

The group started Fairchild Semiconductor in Palo Alto, California, with each founder putting in $500 in seed capital in 1957. They worked on many different versions of microprocessors, eventually bringing to market an integrated circuit and sold millions of them to NASA. The company secured military contracts for cameras and other instruments.

Fairchild's prowess at getting more transistors into each chip led to a consistently powerful low-cost processor. The firm's R&D Director, Gordon Moore, is known for his "law" that predicts a doubling of transistors and resistors on a chip every 24 months.

Fairchild's performance waned a few years later, and the company was sold off. Many of the eight had already moved on. However, some of Fairchild's spinouts became so successful that they started to dominate the market.

The Fairchildren

Fairchild is perhaps better known for its famous "Fairchildren," including Intel, Advanced Micro Devices, and many others. These spinouts inherited the parent's knowledge of how to design and manufacture microprocessors. Complex manufacturing processes are difficult to replicate and are a primary driver of competitiveness in the industry. Some of the Fairchildren got funding from Robert Noyce, a founder of Fairchild Semiconductor. Noyce went on to cofound Intel.[26] Over 160 chip companies are Fairchild spinouts.[27]

---

[25] *IEEE Journals & Magazine | IEEE Xplore*. March 1, 2010. "A Company of Legend: The Legacy of Fairchild Semiconductor." https://ieeexplore.ieee.org/abstract/document/5430761/

[26] Computer History Museum. October 9, 2019. "Fairchildren—CHM," *CHM*. https://computerhistory.org/fairchildren/

[27] Tluong. September 25, 2019. "Fairchild, Fairchildren, and the Family Tree of Silicon Valley," *CHM*. https://computerhistory.org/blog/fairchild-and-the-fairchildren

Implications

- Strategic disagreements about short-term versus long-term objectives can trigger spinouts.
- Abrasive leadership styles can encourage spinouts by increasing dissatisfaction.
- Sometimes spinouts outperform their parents by causing a brain drain.

CHAPTER 7

Spinout Challenges

Entrepreneurs, in general, face many challenges in starting a new business. These include access to capital, lack of experience, and lack of legitimacy, albeit some spinout founders may be able to overcome these obstacles more easily than others. However, for spinout founders, there are other rough waters to navigate in the form of opportunity costs, work–life balance, restrictive covenants, chilling effects, fiduciary duties, and intellectual property rights.

Opportunity Costs

Missing out on the potential benefits of other alternatives is the opportunity cost associated with the selected option. Opportunity costs are often overlooked as they are not incurred by definition, but their identification can improve decision making.[1] A big deterrent to spinouts is the opportunity cost of leaving employment. For example, companies that offer generous benefits may be more expensive to quit.

One might have a secure, comfortable job with a regular salary and benefits. Leaving to do a spinout is a much less certain pathway. Many people rely on employer-sponsored medical insurance and benefits, have health issues, and families to support. Entrepreneurs usually have to pay for their own expensive insurance and have no retirement benefits or pension plans.

Loss of a regular income could mean missing mortgage payments and lead to financial ruin. Few jurisdictions offer insurance for entrepreneurs,

---

[1] J. Fernando. March 17, 2023. "Opportunity Cost Formula, Calculation, and What It Can Tell You," *Investopedia*. www.investopedia.com/terms/o/opportunitycost.asp

such as unemployment benefits. France is one exception—they do insure entrepreneurs in financial distress. But most countries do not offer a similar lifeline. Canada in 2022 launched a voluntary employment insurance program for the self-employed individuals that provides some coverage.[2]

While it may be possible for a founder to take a salary from the business, usually it is not unless and until profitable sales are being made, or deep-pocketed investors come on board to bankroll the management team. We have heard many stories about saving startup capital by working two jobs or living with parents. Much of this stored wealth is to live while starting the business. Alternatively, for many, keeping a day job may be the only way to subsidize the venture at first. One founder explained:

> I learned a ton from my employer, no question, but not like a specific skill, just sharpen all my skill sets and for the really underling goal was to learn as much as could as quickly as could, but just give myself a financial footing where I could jump and start my own thing. In my mind I was ready to jump and start my own thing when I had my salary, like I could live for a year with no salary that I needed and I had another salary set aside for another first employee. (Author interview, Founder 14)

Work–Life Balance

Entrepreneurial stress and lack of work–life balance are potential issue that employees need to deal with when they become entrepreneurs. Startups can require long hours and dedication from their founders, which can make it difficult to keep up with other aspects of life that need attention. Studies show that entrepreneurs' well-being can be negatively affected by hindrance stressors. These can include "role conflicts, interpersonal and work–family conflict, role ambiguity, constraints, work overload, and lack

---

2 Government of Canada. April 6, 2023. "EI Benefits for Self-Employed People: What This Program Offers," *Canada.ca*. www.canada.ca/en/services/benefits/ei/ei-self-employed-workers.html

of necessary resources or support."[3] Entrepreneurs need to develop coping mechanisms to deal with stress. For example, although the work of an entrepreneur doesn't end at 5 p.m., those entrepreneurs who learn to stop working at 5 p.m. have lower stress levels and better work–life balance.

Restrictive Covenants

Restrictive covenants are formal institutions regulating employee mobility and entrepreneurship. Three main types of restrictive covenants are especially relevant for employee entrepreneurs: noncompetes, nonsolicitations, and nondisclosures. Restrictive covenants are placed in employment contracts as well as other types of contracts, like partnerships.

Noncompete Agreements

Probably the most common restrictive covenant is the *noncompete*. A promise not to compete tries to prevent a former employee from going to a competitor or becoming a new competitor. Restrictions typically last for some time (e.g., one year), apply to a specific geography (e.g., a city or state), and defined business activities (e.g., carpet cleaning services). Noncompetes are customary for knowledge workers and managers.[4] They are also used to control lower-level employees in service industries like food service.[5] For example, for many years, until 2016, when the practice was held by a court to be abusive, U.S.-based Jimmy John's had its sandwich makers sign noncompetes, barring them for two years from working for any other sandwich-related business within two miles of a Jimmy John's store.[6]

---

[3] S. Gaonkar and M. Moeen. 2023. "Standing on the Parent's Shoulder or in Its Shadow? Alliance Partner Overlap Between Employee Spinouts and Their Parents," *Strategic Management Journal* 44, no. 2, pp. 415–440.

[4] M. Marx. 2011. "The Firm Strikes Back: Non-Compete Agreements and the Mobility of Technical Professionals," *American Sociological Review* 76, no. 5, pp. 695–712.

[5] J.M. McAdams. 2019. "Non-compete Agreements: A Review of the Literature" Available at SSRN 3513639.

[6] S. Whitten. June 22, 2016. "Jimmy John's Drops Noncompete Clauses Following Settlement," *CNBC*. www.cnbc.com/2016/06/22/jimmy-johns-drops-non-compete-clauses-following-settlement.html

Research shows that strong noncompete enforcement curtails entrepreneurship.[7] Noncompete acts as a screen on spinouts, reducing those that are intra-industry but not much affecting inter-industry spinouts.[8] One founder describes his experience as follows:

> I worked with a bunch of people that I really liked and there was a couple of piece, one was non-competition which because they were a consulting service type development company means I couldn't go out and get a customer that they theoretically have gone after as well, which is ridiculous, it was a crappy contract. I was young and I even didn't fully understand what is happening, so non-competition was part of it. Another one was non-solicitation, so the other people who I worked with all left that company at the same time and said you know what we all wanna work together some day, we know we can't do it right now, we gonna be careful about what we do next couple of years and then we will work on stuff together. That's what we've done. (Author interview, Founder 14)

This founder told us after leaving their job, "I just had to get out into something completely unrelated, if I want to have my own business in that field, so I did." They took a sales job, and after the noncompete expired, he started his own company.

Nondisclosure Agreements

Nondisclosure agreements (NDAs) are widespread in employment and shareholder agreements. By signing an NDA, an employee agrees to keep the organization's confidential information secret. The employee may

---

[7] E. Starr, J. Frake, and R. Agarwal. 2019. "Mobility Constraint Externalities," *Organization Science* 30, no. 5, pp. 961–980.

[8] E. Starr, N. Balasubramanian, and M. Sakakibara. 2018. "Screening Spinouts? How Noncompete Enforceability Affects the Creation, Growth, and Survival of New Firms," *Management Science* 64, no. 2, pp. 552–572.

face legal consequences for giving company secrets to a new employer, selling them to a competitor, or forming a spinout with or around the proprietary information. Spinout lawsuits often turn on whether the information was transferred or whether the spinout made use of it in some material way. These cases commonly involve client lists, company datasets, input cost sheets, or price lists. There are variants of NDAs, such as nondisparagement covenants, that muzzle the employee to prevent them from communicating anything negative about their current or former employer.

Some jurisdictions have adopted a doctrine of inevitable disclosure that assumes a leaver will share their knowledge with their new employer or spinout. This view holds that a former employee is incapable of keeping the employer's secrets. So far, around half of U.S. states have adopted this law, making them inhospitable, even hostile toward spinouts. The doctrine permits the plaintiff in a trade secrets case to establish threatened misappropriation by showing that the defendant's new employment will inevitably lead the defendant to rely on the plaintiff's trade secrets. If a court is satisfied that the doctrine applies in a particular case, it could issue an injunction to prevent the defendant from taking the new job with a competitor, including a spinout.

In most other jurisdictions and most countries, the onus is on the owner of the confidential information, that is, the employer, to prove that a prohibited disclosure occurred, by whom, and what harm resulted from the breach. This is a much greater hurdle for parent firms to clear and serves as a deterrent to using NDAs frivolously rather than for a bona fide purpose.

Nonsolicitation Agreements

Nonsolicitation agreements are used to shield a firm's human resources and customers in the wake of a spinout. They seek to prevent former employees from directly or indirectly poaching the parent's customers or employees. Something as simple as a leaver handing out new business cards to customers and workers on the way out the door would constitute a solicitation.

Nonsolicitation covenants may suck the air out of a ringleader who yearns on taking other employees or customers with them, especially those that would serve as a springboard for the new business.

For example, in the popular television series *Mad Men*, scheming ad executives are able to spirit away with the parent firm's major client, leaving a gaping hole in the parent's revenues. In the world of make-believe, the scoundrels get away with it by having their manager fire them (he was in on the scheme), thus releasing them from their restrictive covenants. A word to the wise: Avoiding your contractual obligations is not so easy in the real world.

Chilling Effects

Cognitive and normative institutions are embodied in organizational culture and can be affected by the leadership of organizations. A chilling effect is when people avoid a legitimate activity because they think there may be legal or normative consequences. In the employee entrepreneurship context, a chilling effect is fearing an aggressive response by one's employer due to its well-known antagonism toward spinouts.[9] For example, a parent firm reputed to engage in litigation or direct other hostility toward leavers.

The chilling effect is a normative belief system held by employees that dissuades them from doing spinouts. Labeling leavers as "traitors" is consistent with an organizational culture that emphasizes loyalty to the employer over other values. An overbearing workplace culture discourages permissible thoughts of setting out on a new career venture.

Ringleader activities in organizations, industries, or jurisdictions with strong chilling effects may be tenuous at best. Some "faithful" employees may view any shop talk of doing a spinout as disloyal conduct and report it to upper management. A workplace with a pronounced chilling effect is less likely to result in backroom or water cooler chatter that puts the

---

[9] M. Marx. 2011. "The Firm Strikes Back: Non-Compete Agreements and the Mobility of Technical Professionals," *American Sociological Review* 76, no. 5, pp. 695–712.

employer in an unflattering light. Employees may not trust each other in this environment, fearing that voicing future aspirations will get them in trouble with the boss.

Curious things happen when we talk to employees and managers about spinouts. Some of them immediately turn defensive, as if the mere mention of the word is taboo. Others have a negative reaction to their entrepreneurial peers leaving to form spinouts. They see it as a loss to their current employer and, by extension, to themselves. A spinout often means an immediate loss of human resources that are difficult to replace or may require those who stay to work overtime to offset the loss. Even if a person is not primarily motivated by loyalty, they may believe it is inherently wrong to take away resources from the employer based on their personal understanding or misunderstanding, as the case may be, of property rights. For instance, some employees who sign noncompetes may believe such promises are morally binding, even if they are not legally enforceable.

Interestingly, chilling effects are greater for some groups than for others, suggesting that they can exacerbate existing disparities and inequalities.

Examining all workers who were employed exclusively within 25 states and the District of Columbia from 1990 to 2014, I find that women subject to tighter non-compete policies were less likely to leave their employers and start rival businesses. Non-competes increase the risk of entrepreneurship by making it harder to hire talent with relevant experience, shifting women away from higher potential ventures. A review of thousands of filed lawsuits suggests that firms do not target women in non-compete cases. Rather, it appears that non-competes disproportionately discourage women from leveraging their professional networks in hiring the sort of talent necessary for high-growth startups to succeed. (Marx 2022, 1756)[10]

---

[10] M. Marx. 2022. "Employee Non-Compete Agreements, Gender, and Entrepreneurship," *Organization Science* 33, no. 5, pp. 1756–1772.

Fiduciary Responsibilities

[A] fiduciary obligation refers to a relationship in which one party (the fiduciary) is responsible for looking after the best interests of another party (the beneficiary). The courts have determined that a fiduciary obligation exists where the fiduciary can exercise some discretion or power, and they do so in a way that affects the interests of the beneficiary. In these relationships, the beneficiary is in a position of vulnerability at the hands of the fiduciary.[11]

In most "common law" countries, employees may have fiduciary responsibilities toward their employers. Duty of care, the duty of loyalty, and the duty of honesty are part of what are today called fiduciary duties that are assigned to directors of corporations, who are typically senior managers or executives. Some lower-ranking employees can also be considered fiduciaries depending on their "access to highly sensitive information or [...] extremely close relationship with certain customers or clients."[12]

Unlike other employees, managers and executives are held to a higher standard of care regarding the interests of the organization's stakeholders, especially investors. As a result, it is even more important that the high-ranking leaver avoid any type of unfair competition as they are much more vulnerable to enforcement of restrictive covenants.

Unlike covenants written into an employment contract, fiduciary responsibilities are automatically assigned to directors in many jurisdictions like Canada[13] and the United Kingdom but also in many U.S. states and beyond. There is no easy way to defend against allegations of a breach of fiduciary duties. Most legal contests turn on whether the leavers had access to or were the "whole show" regarding the business or unit.

---

[11] "Law of Fiduciary Obligation | The Canadian Encyclopedia." 2023. www.thecanadianencyclopedia.ca/en/article/law-of-fiduciary-obligation (accessed March 15, 2023).

[12] W.S. Lazar, G.R. Siniscalco, T.J. Darby, V.G. Oscar De La Vega, and D.J. Millstone. 2023. "Restrictive Covenants and Trade Secrets in Employment Law: An International Survey: Americas, Asia, Middle East and Africa, Oceania," ISBN 9781570189357.

[13] S. Samila and O. Sorenson. 2011. "Noncompete Covenants: Incentives to Innovate or Impediments to Growth," *Management Science* 57, no. 3, pp.425–438.

Larger corporations usually are not satisfied with relying on common law principles to safeguard their business interests. They double down by spelling out a manager's or executive's specific fiduciary duties in an employment contract. For example, a duty of honesty would require the executive to disclose an intention to pursue a spinout.

A duty of care might imply that the spinout founders will be responsible for any losses suffered by the company. A duty of loyalty implies that directors must avoid actions that could be perceived as disloyal to their principals, including the board of directors and investors. To avoid stepping into a fiduciary quagmire, managers and executives planning a spinout are well advised to disclose their intentions, attempt to negotiate some acceptable arrangement with the company, and avoid direct competition with the parent's products.

Intellectual Property Rights

Many countries are members of the World Intellectual Property Organization and work to harmonize their IPR systems to facilitate trade. The Trade-Related Aspects of Intellectual Property Rights (TRIPS) system of the World Trade Organization is also widely adopted.[14] These agreements ensure that intellectual property rights can be extended and enforced in member countries by foreign multinationals.

Our purpose here is not to go into any depth about intellectual property rights but only to briefly discuss how IPR could affect employee entrepreneurs.

Copyrights

Copyrights were historically designed to protect books from being copied without permission. Today, every text that an organization produces is also covered under copyright automatically and immediately after it is created.

---

[14] "WTO | Understanding the WTO—Intellectual Property: Protection and Enforcement." 2023. www.wto.org/english/thewto_e/whatis_e/tif_e/agrm7_e. htm (accessed March 15, 2023).

Copyrights can be relevant for spinout entrepreneurs in some limited cases. A spinout may tangle with copyrights if they reuse the wording, pamphlets of information, manuals, or marketing materials about a product or service from the parent organization. A spinout founder could face allegations of copyright infringement if they reused written materials from their parent firms without permission. For instance, the text on a product manual or promotion might be reused by a zealous entrepreneur who cannot afford their own copy or prefers to save the expense.

Trademarks

Trademarks are meant to protect the identity of the parent organization and its products. They cover things like the names, logos, and colors associated with brands. Trademarks also only apply in limited cases involving counterfeiting of parent firm products. For example, spinout founders learn to make a product and sell knockoff versions of the parent-branded products.

One can imagine a spinout impersonating the parent to profit from customers who do not know any better or do not care. This is akin to counterfeiting in a black market. However, most spinouts avoid imitating their parents down to the exact content, logo, and brand. Those who cross the line perhaps do so out of desperation, thinking that in order to sell to skeptical customers, it is necessary to pass off their products as those of a successful brand. Of course, doing so invites a costly lawsuit.

Trade Secrets

Many important innovations are not protected by patents or copyrights and have, at best, limited protection via trade secret laws. In principle, trade secret law will protect employers from having their employees "steal" confidential information. In practice, detection is problematic and court challenges against former employees are difficult to win (Anton and Yao 1995, 362).[15]

---

[15] J.J. Anton and D.A. Yao. 1995. "Start-Ups, Spin-Offs, and Internal Projects," *The Journal of Law, Economics, and Organization* 11, no. 2, pp. 362–378.

Companies often keep their most sensitive innovations to themselves, safeguarding them as trade secrets with NDAs that limit spillovers. Unlike patents, trade secrets are not published nor submitted for assessment. They are typically enforced by state or provincial-level courts.

Trade secrets cover information that is commercially valuable, that limited people know about, and that has been protected with NDAs and other methods safeguarding information.[16]

Unlike patents and trademarks that must be submitted for official regulatory approval, trade secrets are like copyrights in that they arise automatically. Trade secret protection usually applies as long as the organization can demonstrate to a court that a reasonable effort was made to protect the information in question.

Patents

The most relevant intellectual property rights for many high-tech spinout founders are those issued by a jurisdiction's patent office. Patents have been widely institutionalized in most countries as a legal mechanism to protect their incumbent companies from spinouts.

Patents were invented to create incentives to share and exploit innovations. These are not cash incentives but rather rights. For example, if a king wanted a bridge built but could not pay for it, property rights could be awarded to the architect for designing the bridge. Though the architect received no money upfront, he had the exclusive right for say, 20 years, to profitably rent out the design to others. In modern practice, patent holders charge competitors license fees for replicating their patented design elements.

Patent holders own the rights to tax competitors/customers for the use of the invention, which is documented with images and text in a (normally) public document available from the patent office and online repositories. Patents give the holder the right to take legal action to recover unpaid license fees or otherwise stop the unauthorized use of the proprietary technology.

---

[16] "Trade Secrets." 2023. www.wipo.int/tradesecrets/en/ (accessed March 15, 2023).

A peculiar feature of patents is that most are owned by corporations, not individuals or inventors.[17] When a company employee, say an engineer, makes an invention that leads to a patent, the employer becomes the assignee or owner of the patent, not the employee. The employee is recognized as the inventor but has no rights to the invention. Only the company may license the patent without any further involvement by the inventor. Thus, the patent system is intended to separate ownership from labor.

The types of patent rights continue to expand, such as but not limited to "design patents" that can cover seemingly trivial things like the curvature of a screen or the placement of a button. "Business methods" patents are very broad in their application. They cover activities and processes such as online support systems, money transfer with a unique identifier, quality control of electronic prescriptions, cash management accounts, single-click e-commerce, matching clients with insurance companies, behavioral profiling, and prepaid cellular phones.

Emerging patent rights are in addition to traditional uses to protect inventions in mechanical engineering, electrical engineering, and chemistry. The patent system now covers biotechnology, including most forms of synthetic life. Patents have been applied to pharmaceuticals using the indication logic, that is, if a drug is used for a new purpose, its patent can be renewed for an additional four years. The extensive use of robust patents in the drug industry has made spinouts nearly impossible to execute without buying a license from the company holding the patent.

A controversial development is the software patent, which can cover a myriad of algorithmic creations. These patents can be problematic and difficult to enforce. Software patents can have benefits, like encouraging public disclosure of innovations and protecting some small companies, but they also have many potential disadvantages. They include encouraging patent thickets that hinder research and development activities and innovation, encouraging trivial patents and patent trolls that push

---

[17] A.O. Laplume, E. Xavier-Oliveira, P. Dass, and R. Thakur. 2015. "The Organizational Advantage in Early Inventing and Patenting: Empirical Evidence From Interference Proceedings," *Technovation* 43, pp. 40–48.

them, and creating long delays due to pendencies. Some argue that software patents disproportionately harm startups that are targeted by patent trolls.[18] However, these problems may be more acute in some places than in others. The Netflix movie *Patent Scam* tells the story of several entrepreneurs faced with crippling litigation costs after being targeted by patent trolls.

Parent organizations can try to wall off their intellectual property from spinouts using patents. For example, Blackberry litigated against Kik, accusing it of patent infringement after Kik's messenger service launched. This lawsuit made it difficult for Kik to raise capital as the prospect of an expensive patent suit scared off potential investors. While patents are more relevant in some industries than in others, the increasing breadth and coverage of the institutions is a cause for concern. Jurisdictions with high rates of patent enforcement are particularly perilous, which is why some startups register their businesses where the laws are more favorable.

Negotiate a License

Some spinout founders negotiate a license with the parent organization to use their IP legitimately. In some cases, it may be possible to secure an Intellectual Property Release from the employer upon exit if there is a good relationship between the leaver and the parent's managers. An IP release identifies the type of IP that the leaver may use and the associated conditions to be met. This often includes any prototypes that may have been developed by the leaver. An IP release is similar to a licensing agreement or technology transfer agreement, but it does not specify payment terms.

The IP release might be given in exchange for signing on to certain restrictive covenants or instead of receiving severance pay.

---

[18] J. Bessen. 2014. "The Evidence Is in: Patent Trolls Do Hurt Innovation," *Harvard business review*, pp. 1–4. https://hbr.org/2014/07/the-evidence-is-in-patent-trolls-do-hurt-innovation

Kik and RIM: From Internship to Spinout

Spinout founders may emerge from any rank in the organization. The Kik story shows how a parent firm relationship can sour and lead to litigation. It is also about Ted Livingston, a resilient founder and CEO, who perseveres despite seemingly insurmountable challenges.

Founder Background

As a kid, Livingston spent a lot of time playing with his Legos, perhaps foreshadowing his future in building companies. He grew up in Toronto and studied robotics at the University of Waterloo, in a region dubbed Canada's Silicon Valley that includes campuses for Google, SAS, Ford, D2L, OpenText, and many others.

Livingston received a co-op internship at Research in Motion (RIM), where he became Systems Engineering Project Coordinator and Technical Product Management Coordinator, met product managers, and learned about business.[19] He also found time to create a new software program, Kik, which would interface text messages between BlackBerry and iPhones.[20]

Rather than returning to classes or taking a job after his co-op term ended, Livingston joined the University of Waterloo's Velocity incubator, where he continued to work on the messaging app Kik.

Strategic Disagreements

Although originally developed while a co-op student, Livingston's ambitions for Kik as a platform soon exceeded his employer's interest in the tool. RIM did not want the additional features he wanted to attract a younger audience; social features like groups and search for friends.

---

[19] Annasha. August 14, 2019. "Ted Livingston : The Journey of the Founder of Kik Messenger—Your Tech Story," *Your Tech Story*. www.yourtechstory.com/2019/08/14/ted-livingston-journey-founder-kik-messenger/

[20] P. Winsa and P. Winsa. March 15, 2016. "How Ted Livingston Went From RIM Reject to Kik Starter," *Thestar.Com*. www.thestar.com/news/insight/2016/03/13/how-ted-livingston-went-from-rim-reject-to-kik-starter.html

These aspects may have seemed to compete with and decouple from BlackBerry's contact lists. Kik also offered anonymity as a core feature, with only an e-mail needed for signup.

The conflict between Livingston and RIM reached its peak when RIM removed Kik from its app store and then filed a lawsuit alleging patent infringement and misuse of the parent firm's proprietary information that he had acquired as an employee.[21] The case was eventually settled out of court, and none of the allegations were admitted. However, the suit made it difficult for Livingston to raise funds from traditional investors. Yet, in 2015, Kik served almost half of the U.S. teen messaging market.[22] Eventually, Livingston decided to raise funds using an initial coin offering, an epic success for the venture, raising $100 million.

Outcomes

A few years later, Kik was sued by the U.S. Securities and Exchange Commission (SEC) for its unorthodox fundraising methods. Livingston had vowed to fight the SEC and raised money through crowdfunding to pay for legal costs. He argued the SEC's actions were stifling innovation, making his dispute very public by publishing his response to the SEC.[23] The case was recently settled for five million dollars.

After several controversies, Livingston shut down Kik in 2019, but it continues to be used as freeware for in-game chat. He decided to steer his energies toward Kin, the cryptocurrency. The pivot seems to have paid off as the business continues to attract gaming companies that use Kin as an in-game currency.[24]

---

[21] "Kik Eager to Move on After Settling Spat With BlackBerry." April 10, 2020. *Therecord.Com*. www.therecord.com/news/waterloo-region/2013/10/09/kik-eager-to-move-on-after-settling-spat-with-blackberry.html

[22] "Ted Livingston (Kik)." January 20, 2023. *Wikipedia*. https://en.wikipedia.org/wiki/Ted_Livingston_(Kik)

[23] www.prnewswire.com/news-releases/kik-responds-to-sec-complaint-300862114.html

[24] Kin. October 13, 2022. "Infinity Games Chooses Kin Cryptocurrency for New Web3 Initiative," *Benzinga*. www.benzinga.com/markets/cryptocurrency/22/10/29250497/infinity-games-chooses-kin-cryptocurrency-for-new-web3-initiative

After some financial success, Livingston decided to give back to the incubator that had helped him along the way. With his help, Velocity provides seed capital for startups graduating from its accelerator program—the Velocity Fund Finals competition.[25]

Implications

- Spinout founders may emerge from any level of an organization.
- Use of technology developed for the parent can lead to hostility.
- Although Kik faced litigation, it prevailed and went on to considerable success.

[25] M. Simpson. November 26, 2019. "Velocity Startups Surpass $1 Billion in Total Funding." https://betakit.com/velocity-startups-surpass-1-billion-in-total-funding/ (accessed December 3, 2023).

CHAPTER 8

Spinout Fallout

Up to this point, we have discussed the many advantages of doing a spinout both for the founders and the parent company. However, it is necessary to fairly balance these benefits with potential failure scenarios, which may occur if aspiring entrepreneurs are unable to skillfully manage the relationship with their employers. These scenarios may involve legal, career, and reputational consequences.

Parent Organization Hostility

Some parents are friendly, even welcoming toward spinouts. They may invest in the spinout, license their technology to the spinout, or become their partner. However, other parents are hostile, even belligerent, toward spinouts.

Some organizations purposely cultivate their reputation for toughness by reacting negatively to every suspected infringement of restrictive covenants. They are litigious and want their employees to know it. These parents may take an agency perspective on spinouts where employees, especially managers, are viewed as potential competitors and closely monitored.[1] This perspective may become so extreme that even benign spinouts that could not possibly threaten the parent's interests are unwelcome.

In this section, we examine two questions about parent hostility: (1) What instigates hostility? (2) What are the consequences of parent hostility?

---

[1] T. Hellmann. 2007. "When Do Employees Become Entrepreneurs?" *Management Science* 53, no. 6, pp. 919–933.

Parent Hostility Instigators

> [T]he extent to which employee [spinouts] can access and exploit these resources depends on their parents' goodwill … and not all parent organizations are equally supportive. In fact, the founding of an employee [spinout] often elicits hostile reactions by the parent. (Vaznyte et al. 2021, 268)[2]

Even parent firms that are benevolent toward most spinouts may turn sour under certain conditions and react resentfully. This is more likely if the spinout team had access to proprietary information, transferred it, or used it in the spinout. Another instigator is poaching employees and customers away from the parent firm. Of course, directly competing with the parent firm could also elicit a harsh response.

Using Proprietary Information

Spinout founders that use parent firm proprietary information without authorization may be more likely to face parent company litigation. For example, a parent may be worried about leaking trade secrets through employee mobility. Apple went after Gerard Williams III, who left the company after a long tenure and had planned some aspects of his spinout while employed by Apple. In a counterclaim, Williams demonstrated that the parent obtained his private messages, although he could not show how.[3] In another case, Apple litigated against an early-stage startup that attracted former Apple engineers,[4] showing it would play rough with any attempts to transfer its proprietary information.

---

[2] E. Vaznyte, P. Andries, and S. Demeulemeester. 2021. "'Don't Leave Me This Way!' Drivers of Parental Hostility and Employee Spin-Offs' Performance," *Small Business Economics* 57 pp. 265–293.

[3] R. Kaser. December 12, 2019. "Former Employee Says Apple Spied on His Private Messages," *TNW|Apple*. https://thenextweb.com/news/former-employee-says-apple-spied-on-his-private-messages

[4] Dazeinfo. July 28, 2022. "Apple Has Sued Just a Year-Old Startup: A Warning Message to All Startups," *Dazeinfo*. https://dazeinfo.com/2022/05/03/why-apple-suing-just-a-year-old-startup-is-kind-of-a-big-deal/

Soliciting Employees and Customers

> They didn't go after him [cofounder] or me [ringleader], but when
> we hired the engineers ... [that] upset them. And they had six
> counts against us and they served the warrants at 10 o'clock at
> night in our homes. The idea was to scare us and more impor-
> tantly, to scare away the money because the deal hadn't closed....
> The lawsuit ended up getting dropped later, because it wasn't
> successful in doing what they wanted it to do, which was scare
> people away, scare the money away (Shah et al. 2019, 1440)[5]

Taking employees and customers away from the parent increases the
parent's estimation of loss. For example, the parent must deal with replacing personnel and somehow compensate for lost sales. Some parents try
to use litigation to hang onto their human resources. In *Apple v. Gerard
Williams*, the plaintiff accused him of unlawfully encouraging employees
to leave to join a start-up.[6]

Competing With the Parent

Spinouts can confront their parents by going to market with competing
products. Even indirect competition with substitute products can take a
chunk out of the parent's bottom line, mainly when it affects the parent's
ability to keep or achieve a competitive advantage. Spinouts that overlap substantially with the parent's product markets will likely encounter
pushback.

Consequences of Hostility for Spinouts

Parent retaliation is one of the most important factors limiting employee
entrepreneurship. That can lower the spinout's performance by making

---

[5] S.K. Shah, R. Agarwal, and R. Echambadi. 2019. "Jewels in the Crown: Exploring the Motivations and Team Building Processes of Employee Entrepreneurs,"
Strategic Management Journal 40, no. 9, pp. 1417–1452.

[6] C. Wood. December 10, 2019. "Apple is Suing Its Former Lead Chip Designer
After He Quit to Set up His Own Chip Company," *Business Insider*. www
.businessinsider.com/apple-suing-ex-employee-after-he-quit-tech-giant-2019-12

it harder to raise capital, cover expenses, and pay focused attention to the business. Trouble raising capital means less scale for growth and can reduce the chances of survival.

Legal expenses likely will be substantial, reducing cash flow for other business expenses needed for firm growth and survival. A lawsuit creates a significant distraction that prevents the spinout from operating optimally.

Parent organizations usually have deeper pockets to sustain a legal fight. Litigation is expensive for both parties but tends to be disproportionately burdensome for the leavers unless the parent is small or insolvent.

After being served with notice of litigation, one can ignore it but does so at their peril. A court judgment could result in a fine, an order to pay damages, or other reparations to the parent organization. However, a court would more likely issue an injunction forbidding activities that breach restrictive covenants. Courts can enforce injunctions by authorizing search and seizure of property and even arrests. Injunctions are usually reasonably narrow, making it possible for the spinout to continue doing business in other areas.

Most disputes are settled out of court. The details of these settlements are rarely disclosed; however, they often result in a spinout paying a sum of money to the parent. This may be for a license to use proprietary technology or as a negotiated amount to compensate for the harm caused to the parent by the spinout's prohibited activities.

A parent may withdraw a case if there is insufficient evidence to support its claims or simply decide that the cost of a legal battle is not worthwhile. But it is important to remember that the sheer cost of a spinout's defense may have already taken a serious financial toll.

Beyond legal problems, getting blacklisted by the parent organization can potentially affect a spinout's ability to recruit human resources, attract investors, and source supplier inputs. For example, a recent study found that spinouts who sell products in the same markets as their parents are more likely to have to find new strategic alliance partners. By contrast, spinouts that do not compete, but still build on parent firm technology, are more likely to share alliance partners with their parents.[7] This kind of

---

[7] K. Walsh, J. Nelles, and S. Stephens. 2023. "Recycling in Entrepreneurial Ecosystems: The Phenomenon of Boomeranging," *R&D Management*.

problem might be more acute in a "one horse town," where the parent has real, local power (e.g., it is an anchor firm); the company might persuade its stakeholders to avoid doing business with the spinout. Prospective employees might also be shy about joining a blacklisted spinout for fear of being similarly treated. We cover how entrepreneurs avoid these pitfalls in Chapter 9.

In the Event of Failure

Despite having distinct advantages over other types of startups due to their inheritance, spinouts are not guaranteed success. They can fail for many of the same reasons as other startups, including lack of product market fit and poor execution. They may also fail due to parent organization influence, hostile activities, or litigation, all factors that other startups do not face.

Can the team return to work for the parent organization if the spinout fails? Probably not. Bridges have been burned, especially by spinout ringleaders who have been stamped as persona non grata. All but the most spinout-friendly parents will not want them back in the fold. The research suggests that entrepreneurs behind failing spinouts may have dimmer employment prospects in general.[8] However, the so-called "boomerang" career, where entrepreneurs are recycled back into employment somewhere within the entrepreneurial ecosystem, is becoming more common.[9]

One way to avoid a new venture's pitfalls is to keep working for the parent company until the side-hustle business model is fully validated (i.e., hybrid entrepreneurship). This approach bucks the popular rhetoric about heroic entrepreneurship, needing to *go all in*, feeling *the fear*, or having faith in yourself to take extraordinary risks.

Hybrid entrepreneurship is less risky and less stressful. Researchers have examined hybrid entrepreneurs' performance and find that

---

[8] O. Kacperczyk and P. Younkin. 2022. "A Founding Penalty: Evidence From an Audit Study on Gender, Entrepreneurship, and Future Employment," *Organization Science* 33, no. 2, pp. 716–745.
[9] K. Walsh, J. Nelles, and S. Stephens. 2023. "Recycling in Entrepreneurial Ecosystems: The Phenomenon of Boomeranging," *R&D Management*.

they perform better than entrepreneurs who take the plunge earlier.[10] Not only can a day job provide economic stability and even subsidize the startup, but it also allows for a softer landing if the venture does not pan out—one still has their job to fall back on. The evidence suggests that one should not quit their day job until their startup has some traction, assuming that having a side gig isn't expressly forbidden by one's employment contract.

Case Study: Chevrolet

The Chevrolet story is a classic and complex story with unhappy endings for its main protagonists, William Durant and Louis Chevrolet.

Founder Background

William Durant was a millionaire at age 40 after big wins in the insurance industry. He had built a carriage business that grew to employ a vast swath of Flint, Michigan. His love of cars drove him to take on the leadership of Buick.[11] Buick was wildly successful, at one point outselling Ford and Chrysler. Durant was seen as a genius for succeeding first in the carriage business but then also successfully transitioning to the automotive industry, transforming Flint's economy along the way.

Durant then formed a holding company (General Motors) that conducted a number of acquisitions with some being success stories (e.g., Buick and Oldsmobile), but he also made other acquisitions in related industries, like tractors, many of which failed.[12] He even spent millions on a phony patent, wasting company resources.

---

[10] C. Demir, A. Werner, S. Kraus, and P. Jones. 2020. "Hybrid Entrepreneurship: A Systematic Literature Review," *Journal of Small Business and Entrepreneurship* 34, no. 1, pp. 29–52.

[11] "Story of GM Founder William Durant | General Motors." 2023. www.gm.com/heritage/durant (accessed March 15, 2023).

[12] R. Kelly. January 16, 2021. "William Durant Founded GM, Lost It, Took It Back, Lost It Again," *Printers Devil (Blog)*. www.printersdevil.ca/william-durant-founded-gm/

Meanwhile, Louis Chevrolet, at age 21, moved to New York and eventually landed a job at Fiat's U.S. branch in 1905.[13] He was hired as a race car driver and placed on the company racing team, where he learned a great deal about engines.[14] He was no ordinary driver; he was also a technical wiz with excellent knowledge of automobile mechanics. Despite being a racing star, Chevrolet was eventually drawn to a job as a designer in Philadelphia with the Christie automaker. He worked on innovative projects there, including the world's first front-wheel drive systems. His racing prowess and design skills attracted him to a job offer from Durant, who wanted him to market a sporty new car.

Spinout Story

Durant disagreed with GM stakeholders about the value of going after the small car market. They were more interested in growing their large car business.[15]

In 1910, big problems arose. The market for large cars dried up. People were flocking to Henry Ford's reliable and inexpensive Model T, his only model. GM, meanwhile, offered 21 different models of larger cars produced by 10 independent divisions, few of which were profitable. Durant's image went from genius to foolish speculator.[16]

Durant left GM over a strategic disagreement about the company's acquisition strategy. Durant started Chevrolet in 1911 with Chevrolet and others to go after the small car market, essentially leaving his mistakes

---

[13] https://gmauthority.com/blog/2022/06/the-story-of-louis-chevrolet-video/

[14] K. Menon. August 18, 2022. "The Untold Yet Tragic Story of Chevrolet's Co-Founder, Louis Chevrolet," *HotCars*. www.hotcars.com/tragic-story-co-founder-louis-chevrolet/

[15] I. Ioannou. April 1, 2014. "When Do Spinouts Enhance Parent Firm Performance? Evidence From the U.S. Automobile Industry, 1890–1986," *Organization Science* 25, no. 2, pp. 529–551. https://doi.org/10.1287/orsc.2013.0846

[16] "Story of GM Founder William Durant | General Motors." 2023. www.gm.com/heritage/durant (accessed March 15, 2023).

behind. Chevrolet was quite successful. It sold its first production models in 1913 and had increasing sales and profitability.[17]

The spinout was so profitable that Durant could buy enough GM shares to take over the company and install himself as president. Like Buick before it, Chevrolet was acquired and folded into GM and became one of its highest-performing divisions, although it did go through some tumultuous periods.

Outcomes

Conflicts between Chevrolet and Durant, over informal agreements and a restructuring plan imposed without the former's consent, led Chevrolet to sell his stake in the company to Durant. He continued to win races and used the winning to found his own spinout, the Frontenac Motor Company, which eventually failed due to a Wall Street scandal. Chevrolet fell into poverty and never regained fame or position. He purportedly died as a mechanic working on Chevrolet's line.[18]

Back as GM president, Durant started making acquisitions again, angering the board and some key bankers who forced him out of the company once more. He founded Durant Motors (his second spinout) the next day.[19] That company failed in a recession, and Durant had to work his way back. His last known business was a bowling alley.

Implications

- Dissatisfaction with a spinout's trajectory can lead to serial entrepreneurship.
- Spinout founders do not always prosper from their endeavors.

---

[17] Wikipedia contributors. April 8, 2023. "Chevrolet," *Wikipedia.* https://en.wikipedia.org/wiki/Chevrolet

[18] "The Untold Yet Tragic Story of Chevrolet's Co-Founder, Louis Chevrolet." August 18, 2022. *HotCars.* www.hotcars.com/tragic-story-co-founder-louis-chevrolet/.

[19] "William Durant | Automotive Hall of Fame." 2023. www.automotivehallof-fame.org/honoree/william-durant/ (accessed March 15, 2023).

CHAPTER 9

Alternatives

As discussed, employee entrepreneurs face challenges and potential fall-out in their transition to creating their own ventures. According to the literature on strategic responses,[1] possible responses to these issues include defiance, acquiescence, compromise, and avoidance, each with its own pros and cons. Our role is not to recommend any one option but merely to alert the reader as to the facts about each.

Defiance is ignoring all institutional norms and possible consequences, simply charging ahead, and starting the new business. Defiance has been covered in other chapters, so we move on to the other options. The most conservative response is acquiescence.

Acquiescence: Throwing in the Towel

Acquiescence happens merely by following old habits that have become routine or by imitating examples or models set forward as doing right or conforming to norms and following the rules set by local, regional, and national authorities. For employee entrepreneurs, acquiescence means abandoning their business ideas and staying an employee. Those who have acquiesced have plenty of company.

There is a reason why large organizations often have storage cabinets or disks bursting with remnants of discarded innovations. Most new ideas are bad business ideas that should not be pursued. Unfortunately, it can be impossible to know in advance which ideas are good or bad.[2] Some ideas are not good enough to overcome the tall barriers in front of them

---

[1] C. Oliver. 1991. "Strategic Responses to Institutional Processes," *Academy of Management Review* 16, no. 1, pp. 145–179.

[2] J.G. March. 1991. "Exploration and Exploitation in Organizational Learning," *Organization Science* 2, no. 1 pp. 71–87.

and are not worth putting in the time and energy. Another idea could come along later that has a much larger potential payoff. Not chasing a bad idea brings the benefit of freeing one's mind to go after the next better idea.

Discarding the entrepreneurial dream altogether may be the best decision because most new business ideas are risky, the opposite of job security and stability. The turmoil of venture failure and financial problems can also lead to family conflict over decisions and increased social tension, compounding personal problems for sinking entrepreneurs.

Entrepreneurship is not for everyone. It involves stress, uncertainty, and risks that are more significant than those experienced in employment. Business failure is also a real prospect, and it may be more challenging to return to employment or recover financially than just losing a job. Despite the use of limited liability companies, failure can sometimes lead to personal bankruptcy, especially for founders who have borrowed to invest. Shareholders are last in order of priority if a business is wound up and its assets, if any, are distributed by court order. The money usually runs out before investors recover anything. The bankers and employees get paid first. All things considered, investing in startups is not for the faint of heart who naively dream of overnight success.

Finding a Compromising

Compromise is about finding a balance between interests, accommodating, pacifying, or placating. It entails bargaining or negotiating with the employer and its stakeholders. The employee entrepreneur chooses compromise when pursuing the startup internally via intrapreneurship or corporate spinoff.

Intrapreneurship

If the employee innovator can get a sufficient commitment of parent resources, it may be possible to pursue the idea as an internal corporate venture. Intrapreneurship allows employees to pursue company-sanctioned innovations while the parent retains ownership. Intrapreneurship may be the path of least resistance as the employer may already have complementary assets like manufacturing, distribution, and marketing that are needed to go to market successfully, saving considerable time and money. However, intrapreneurship is only truly effective if the parent firm is willing and able to invest sufficiently in the project. Most businesses are unable to fund many new projects and are quick to cut back on these investments during an economic downturn.

Intrapreneurship reduces the downside risk for employees, who likely will stay employed even if the venture does not work out. They get to engage in entrepreneurial behaviors within their comfort zone and with the security of a parent's safety net. But there is a price to be paid for this as choosing intrapreneurship usually requires giving up coveted ownership of the innovation to the parent company.

Some organizations provide entrepreneurial employees with equity-based or performance-based compensation to give them some real skin in the game. Sometimes a contract is negotiated where the employer shares a percentage of the new venture's value with the intrapreneurs. If things do not work out, the employer may allow the innovators to try a different approach or at least return to their regular day jobs more seamlessly. Our own research on this suggests that employees who gain experience doing intrapreneurship for their employers are more likely to strike out on their own later as entrepreneurs.[3]

Finally, research suggests that employees who engage in intrapreneurship activities feel more positively about their jobs.[4] This is perhaps because entrepreneurial tasks offer a high level of autonomy, which corresponds to a basic human need.

Corporate Spinoffs

If the venture is a well-advanced internal corporate venture, there is a team formed and customers are already buying, then a corporate spinoff (a.k.a. starburst) might be appropriate. Unlike an employee spinout, an autonomous process led by employees, a corporate spinoff occurs when

---

[3] S. Yeganegi, A.O. Laplume, P. Dass, and N.S. Greidanus. 2019. "Individual-Level Ambidexterity and Entrepreneurial Entry," *Journal of Small Business Management* 57, no. 4, pp. 1444–1463.

[4] N. Shir, B.N. Nikolaev, and J. Wincent. 2019. "Entrepreneurship and Well-Being: The Role of Psychological Autonomy, Competence, and Relatedness," *Journal of Business Venturing* 34, no. 5, p. 105875.

the parent company's top management decides to hive off a division or business unit from the company. The unit is moved out of the corporation and becomes its own separate corporate entity with its own shares and ticker symbol.

In a corporate spinoff, the parent's investors receive shares in the spinoff proportional to their holdings in the parent's stock. For example, where a parent company might want to be acquired but the buyer only wants the core business, then the peripheral businesses can be packaged into one or more new organizations and spun off separately. Thus, corporate spinoffs are intended to ensure that parent investors are fully compensated.

One advantage of a corporate spinoff is that the whole team can usually exit intact rather than having to reconstruct a viable team to support a spinout. The main drawback is that the intrapreneur remains an employee or manager and gets compensated accordingly. This can mean more stability but also cuts the intrapreneur out of the potential for huge equity growth if things go well for the spinoff company.

Avoiding the Parent

First, a spin-out pursuing network development links up with new partners, including suppliers, customers, and competitors, that are not directly connected to the parent and are thus less likely to be subject to its influences. In doing so, the spin-out reduces its parent's ability to sanction or obstruct it, effectively emancipating itself from its influence (Walter et al. 2014, 2035).[5]

In avoiding the parent entrepreneurial employees explore their ideas externally, spinning out from their current employer organization. However, they try to avoid their parents' hostility. Learning to avoid hazards is a basic human adaptation. By anticipating what may be lurking around the corner, we are more likely to avoid trouble. Therefore, avoiding a likely hostile parent response to a spinout might be a prudent

---

[5] S.G. Walter, S. Heinrichs, and A. Walter. 2014. "Parent Hostility and Spin-Out Performance," *Strategic Management Journal* 35, no. 13, pp. 2031–2042.

option. Avoidance is about loosening attachments or escaping by altering goals and related activities or even changing domains altogether.

Geographic Avoidance

Founders may want to physically locate their spinout far enough away from their parent firm in order to avoid consequences altogether. This can be difficult to do because of ties to family, friends, and local industry networks. However, locating in another jurisdiction where there is less or no chance of any legal fallout is an option to consider. For instance, a strict noncompete signed in Florida or Alberta could not be upheld in California or Ontario. Alternatively, the business could be started outside of the geographic scope of restrictive covenants.

Some spinout founders locate their businesses far away from their parent organizations, even though this can sometimes be a major inconvenience to their family members. Some of the founders we interviewed complained they felt forced to move their business to avoid any potential for conflict with the parent company, often because they had signed multiyear noncompetes that barred them from operating in their preferred city.

Going global from the start, or being born global, is one potential avenue for avoidance. Tapping supply-chain or customer networks in other countries is an alternative. By incorporating in a neutral jurisdiction and moving operations internationally, a spinout can make it more difficult for parent organizations to enforce regionally or nationally bound restrictive covenants.

Market Avoidance

Both the product market and the input factor markets matter. Recent research suggests that spinouts that enter markets that overlap with those of their parents are more likely to face combative parent responses.[6]

---

[6] A. Bahoo-Torodi, and S. Torrisi. 2022. "When Do Spinouts Benefit From Market Overlap With Parent Firms?" *Journal of Business Venturing* 37, no. 6, p. 106249.

This implies another avoidance strategy: developing new networks of customers and suppliers that minimally overlap with those of the parent's networks.

Suppose the spinout sells to different customers and uses alternative suppliers. In that case, even though it can be an intra-industry spinout on the surface, there is no direct competition with the parent and the framing changes.

Research suggests that spinouts benefit the most when they are partially related or similar to their parent companies but also differentiated, both in terms of startup team composition[7] and market overlap with the parent. Similarities allow spinout founders to leverage more from parent firm experiences while exhibiting sufficient differences. Some spinouts could benefit from unlearning some of the less effective routines that they inherited.[8]

Industry Avoidance: Vertical Spinouts

Spinout founders may choose vertical spinout strategies (i.e., starting a spinout in the parent firm's upstream or downstream industry) to achieve their avoidance goals. Going to an upstream or downstream industry reduces head-on competition with the parent. Vertical spinouts also open up the possibility of keeping or developing an ongoing transactional relationship with the parent.[9]

Thus, vertical spinouts can be neutral by being independent new ventures that can become customers or suppliers of their parents. For example, the parent might supply a key input like licensing a technology or providing contract manufacturing to the spinout. The spinout sells to

---

[7] F. Honoré. 2022. "Joining Forces: How Can Founding Members' Prior Experience Variety and Shared Experience Increase Startup Survival?" *Academy of Management Journal* 65, no. 1, pp. 248–272.

[8] S. Ferriani, E. Garnsey, and G. Lorenzoni. 2012. "Continuity and Change in a Spin-Off Venture: The Process of Reimprinting," *Industrial and Corporate Change* 21, no. 4, pp. 1011–1048.

[9] P. Adams, R. Fontana, and F. Malerba. 2019. "Linking Vertically Related Industries: Entry by Employee Spinouts Across Industry Boundaries," *Industrial and Corporate Change* 28, no. 3, pp. 529–550.

the parent organization (supplier-industry spinout). It can also go the other way, where the spinout buys from the parent (customer-industry spinout).

Vertical spinouts are expected to cause less friction with their parents because there is more potential to become economic partners rather than competitors. Ongoing parent-spinout transactions also create value through the exchange of information. This can go a long way to smoothing the relationship, even if the spinout transfers considerable resources from the parent, for example, by luring away employees of the parent firm.

Vertical spinouts highlight that opportunities can come from any part of the value chain. The value chain is a way to think about all the different activities over time that transform raw materials into products used by consumers. This includes procurement, engineering, manufacturing, packaging, marketing, distribution, process improvement, service, and support.

Technological Avoidance

In some industries, patents are airtight (e.g., pharmaceuticals and chemicals). In others, they are leaky (e.g., software) or irrelevant. Without a license, overcoming the parent's strong patents means the spinout may have to use entirely different technology, which could make the venture infeasible.

Avoiding the parent's core technology may be viable in some cases, allowing the spinout to differentiate itself enough to avoid confrontation. Usually, the spinout will either use a newer technology that the parent company has decided not to adopt or failed to adopt. Other times, a spinout may actually be continuing with the older technology as the parent moves on to newer tech.

A promising approach to avoidance is the leapfrogging strategy. The spinout adopts a new generation of technology that is a bleeding edge substitute for that being used by their parent. The new technology will attract more innovative customers while the parent organization continues to chase its existing customer base. Skipping to next-generation technology positions the spinout as an indirect competitor.

Lineage Avoidance

Lineage avoidance may be achieved by combining founders with experience at different companies. A multiparent spinout may alter how parent organizations respond and can respond because of the diluted impact of each parent's inheritance. Each founder may transfer something from their parent, and the team recombines it into something new.

We looked at a dataset of all the startups participating in the Techstars accelerator program and found that many hailed from one, two, or even three parent organizations. Out of the 1,258 startups that participated in the Techstars accelerator program between 2008 and 2019, only a third (n = 434) were by spinout founders with no prior work experience in the last year before becoming a founder (e.g., students). The most frequent number of parents is one (n = 521). But interestingly, the remaining startups had two, three, or four parents (n = 236, 58, 9, respectively).

Many startups have small teams made up of founders who left employment to embark on their new venture. Such multilineage is more likely to be better differentiated from any one parent organization.

Recent research suggests that the best way to gain from the experiences in parent organizations is to add variety to the startup team by adding partners or employees with different backgrounds, including employers.[10] Unique combinations of individuals that connect previously unconnected industry networks create opportunities for entrepreneurs to exploit.

Working for Another Company

If an employer is not interested in an employee's innovation—why not shop it around to competitors that may be interested? Of course, mobility to other companies is an option; however, research shows that it may be suboptimal. Leaving to do a startup provides the benefit of a clean

---

[10] F. Honoré. 2022. "Joining Forces: How Can Founding Members' Prior Experience Variety and Shared Experience Increase Startup Survival?" *Academy of Management Journal* 65, no. 1, pp. 248–272.

slate.[11] Going to work for another incumbent is not at all a clean slate. Odds are the innovator will encounter similar resistance in getting the idea accepted.

This is especially so for complex knowledge, which is difficult to integrate into existing processes. Resistance will be greater still if the new host company has a "not-invented-here" syndrome. The company's routines are so entrenched that everything new has to fit with its routines, otherwise, the innovation gets rejected, or worse, it jams up the host's system. Since it is difficult to buck deep-set routines, innovators may find there is too much friction to overcome. It is likely much easier to start from scratch.

Besides, other incumbents may pass on the idea for the same reasons as the parent firm. In particular, if the innovation threatens an organization's competencies or risks disrupting the industry by creating substitute products, then no one may be interested.

Case Study: 23andMe

23andMe is a new kind of B2C biotechnology firm based in Sunnyvale, California. It provides the general public access to their genetic information in the form of reports about ancestry and predispositions. The name of the company was inspired by the 23 pairs of chromosomes in a normal human cell.[12]

Anne E. Wojcicki graduated from Yale University with a BSc in biology in 1996. In 2006, Wojcicki, with biologists Linda Avey and Paul Cusenza, cofounded 23andMe as a result of her interest in genetic testing's potential to impact the health care industry.[13]

---

[11] M. Ganco. 2013. "Cutting the Gordian Knot: The Effect of Knowledge Complexity on Employee Mobility and Entrepreneurship," *Strategic Management Journal* 34, no. 6, pp. 666–686.

[12] Wikipedia contributors. April 3, 2023. "Anne Wojcicki," *Wikipedia.* https://en.wikipedia.org/wiki/Anne_Wojcicki

[13] K. Rogers. May 3, 2017. "Anne Wojcicki | Biography, Facts, & 23andMe," *Encyclopedia Britannica.* www.britannica.com/biography/Anne-Wojcicki

Where It Began

Before starting 23andMe, Wojcicki worked on Wall Street, where she analyzed the health care industry's companies.

> In some ways, as an analyst on Wall Street, I couldn't have asked for a better training because here I was at 22 and I had this opportunity to study every single healthcare company out there. I always felt like my 10 years on Wall Street was like getting a Ph.D. and then a postdoc, Wojcicki said.[14]

She was frustrated with a health care system that emphasized illness rather than prevention. In various interviews,[15] she laments that the current system seems to be taking advantage of people. In contrast to businesses that make money out of illnesses and treating the symptoms, she wanted to create one that helps people prevent illness in the first place.

During her time on Wall Street, although she enjoyed studying health care organizations, learning the science underlying their work, and speaking with CEOs and even Nobel Prize winners, she lost hope in the health care sector.

Outcomes

In 2008, *Time* magazine named 23andMe's personal genome test kit "Invention of the Year."[16] The startup was able to achieve a valuation of

---

[14] T. Dunn. April 19, 2018. "Anne Wojcicki, CEO of 23andMe, Shares Advice for Entrepreneurs and Overcoming Setbacks," *ABC News*. https://abcnews.go.com/Business/anne-wojcicki-ceo-23andme-shares-advice-entrepreneurs-overcoming/story?id=54587273

[15] Stanford Graduate School of Business. May 23, 2022. "Anne Wojcicki, Co-Founder and CEO of 23andMe." www.youtube.com/watch?v=87GDuh7q6xo

[16] TIME.com. October 29, 2008. "Best Inventions of 2008—TIME." https://content.time.com/time/specials/packages/article/0,28804,1852747_1854493_1854113,00.html

over a billion dollars, thus attaining the fabled unicorn status. The funding came from nearly a dozen top venture capital firms.

After many years of experience, 23andMe claims to have built one of the largest genetic databases, with more than five million customers.[17] In 2018, the company announced that GlaxoSmithKline, a major pharmaceutical company, had invested $300 million to secure exclusive access to the genetic testing startup's DNA database.[18]

Implications

- Spinout founders may change their industry as a result of dissatisfaction with the way an industry operates.
- Employees have the option of inter-industry spinouts.
- By becoming a customer of the parent, a vertical spinout is achieved.

Case Study: Zillow

Zillow's spinout is remarkable because of how it replicated the essential principles of its parent firm but applied them to another industry. Rich Barton graduated from Stanford Engineering, then in the early 90s, went to work at Microsoft as a product manager. Barton founded Expedia within Microsoft as an internal corporate venture. Microsoft eventually spun off the travel firm as a separate company.[19]

---

[17] "Anne Wojcicki, CEO of 23andMe, Shares Advice for Entrepreneurs and Overcoming Setbacks." April 19, 2018. *ABC News.* https://abcnews.go.com/Business/anne-wojcicki-ceo-23andme-shares-advice-entrepreneurs-overcoming/story?id=54587273

[18] *Healthcare IT News.* July 25, 2018. "23andMe Lands $300 Million Investment From GlaxoSmithKline." www.healthcareitnews.com/news/23andme-lands-300-million-investment-glaxosmithkline

[19] Wikipedia contributors. November 20, 2022. "Rich Barton," *Wikipedia.* https://en.wikipedia.org/wiki/Rich_Barton

Strategic Disagreements

In 2003, a large block of Expedia's investors installed a new chairman of the board, who bemoaned a bloated organization and started to press cost reductions.[20] After this change in strategic direction, Barton and his co-worker Frink started thinking about a new venture. Both men had newborn children at home and wanted more space but found it overwhelming to find basic real estate marketplace information.

It was 2005, and the duo thought it was unbelievable that there was no application or website for real estate information except for the Multiple Listing Service (MLS). A year later, they stealthily came up with Zillow as an online market for American real estate. One of the interesting strategies in this startup was the idea behind information transparency. They believed that consumers are more likely to make different decisions when they have access to accurate information. Zillow users get real estate information and are connected to Zillow's partners: real estate agents, financial advisers, construction companies, property management companies, property owners, and land and building services.[21]

Stealthy Spinout

The Zillow concept was influenced by Barton and Frink's first startup, Expedia. If travel choices could be simplified by allowing easier access to information, why not have a website for residential real estate information? Zillow was, in that sense, an extension of Expedia. Interestingly, Barton also cofounded Glassdoor, which uses the same data-driven business model.

Zillow is famous for its "Zestimates," which are home value estimations based on its algorithms and data. It is also controversial because it

---

[20] "Yahoo Is Part of the Yahoo Family of Brands." 2023. https://finance.yahoo.com/news/expedia-chairman-barry-diller-rips-005004976.html (accessed March 15, 2023).

[21] J. Cook. n.d. "Zillow at 10: Rich Barton, Spencer Rascoff and Lloyd Frink on the Rise of the Real Estate Media Titan," www.geekwire.com/2016/zillow-10-years/

can affect housing prices in areas or over- and underprice properties in ways that inadvertently help or harm sellers or buyers. But people love to see what their house is worth, and a Zestimate is free! It helps both buyers and sellers think about what price a property might go for.

Implications

- Changes in company strategy can spur spinout teams.
- Spinout may apply the same technologies as their parent but to new industries.

CHAPTER 10

Spinout Validation

Like other entrepreneurs, spinout founders need to validate their business ideas from the outset. The business model validation process is likely to be experienced differently by spinout founders than it is for other entrepreneurs.

Business Idea Validation

Business idea validation has a central place in entrepreneurship education as it is assumed that many entrepreneurs have a technology or product idea that has not been validated. But they do need to know who their customers are and if those customers will buy their products. Skipping this first step is likely to end in business failure.

In the popular literature on startups, there are references to *crossing the chasm.*[1] This refers to the product life cycle model where the first customers are innovators, followed by early adopters, the early majority, the late majority, and lastly the laggards. The chasm is the gap between what innovators and early adopters are willing to accept and what the early majority is willing to accept. Startups can fail to transition their product from something that early adopters want into something that the early majority will buy.

Geoffrey Moore suggests that the way to span the chasm is to develop the "whole product," that is, rather than building a product for many different customer segments, successful startups concentrate on a single customer segment. This singular objective is risky but also necessary to create the willingness to buy. Choosing the right customer segment has deep implications for the product, including its cost, quality, responsiveness, and reliability. If a startup does not pick one segment to cater to, it can

---

[1] G. Moore. 1991. "Crossing the Chasm," *Harper Business* (New York, NY).

slip into the chasm and never come out—selling a product for everyone that no one wants.

Selecting the wrong customer segment can be a sure way to fail, but failing to select is even worse, producing something that no one wants by trying to cater to disparate interests. Repeated warnings about the need to target a specific segment have led to the development of various techniques that entrepreneurs can employ.

Customer Discovery

Customer segmentation logic is behind much of the entrepreneurship education found today in startup books and online. The emphasis is on finding or discovering who your customers are by testing assumptions about your business model and product. For example, the Lean Launchpad developed by Steve Blank and others is based on helping entrepreneurs figure out how to make a product that customers will want to buy.[2]

To avoid building out the wrong product that few customers will buy, entrepreneurs ought to validate their ideas by talking to people who would be stakeholders in their ventures, especially potential customers.

The process of customer discovery involves interviewing potential customers and other stakeholders, and asking about their problems, needs, and wants. Talking to real people often leads to dropping the original ideas or pivoting to new ones. Recording and transcribing these interviews makes it possible to identify additional themes later through analysis techniques and software tools.

The customer discovery approach has made inroads in North America. For example, it is fundamental to the iCorps program, a federally funded National Science Foundation professional development series taking place on dozens of university campuses across the United States. iCorps exists to expose university scientists and engineers to customer discovery practices to ascertain if there is a market for their innovations before they (and their universities) go down a dead-end path.

---

[2] S. Blank and B. Dorf. 2020. *The Startup Owner's Manual: The Step-by-Step Guide for Building a Great Company* (John Wiley & Sons).

Business Model Canvas

Tools like the business model canvas or startup canvas help guide the process of customer discovery. They are a modern, single-page alternative to the 30-page business plan. Typically, a canvas has eight boxes the entrepreneur fills out to briefly explain their proposed business opportunity. Each box is labeled with some variation of "key partners," "key activities," "key resources," "value propositions," "channels," "cost structure," "revenue streams," and "customer segments."

For example, for a publishing startup, key partners could be book publishers, key activities could be AI-written books, and key resources might be access to the latest chatbots. The value proposition might be a low-cost way to write a custom book on demand. Each book would be unique based on a detailed prompt provided by the reader or customer. Channels could include thousands of botted book promotion websites with direct purchase options. Cost structure would involve counting the costs of developing the organization to support development, maintenance, promotion, and management functions. Revenue streams could include print-on-demand and ebooks, as well as audiobooks. Customer segments might include readers looking for books that address their specific needs or wants. Instead of a book about entrepreneurship, I might want one about entrepreneurship tailored to the vertical gardening industry in northern cities with details about how to turn my living room into a herb garden.

Hypothesis Testing

The entrepreneur makes assumptions or hypotheses in each box of the canvas. The content written into each box is a set of hypotheses to be tested. Thus, the canvas may be viewed as a research program entrepreneurs use to validate their business model or startup. For example, in the "customer segments" box, the entrepreneur may write "high-end customers with a taste for luxury." This is a hypothesis.

A hypothesis is a statement about a relationship between two constructs, an independent variable and a dependent variable, that can be tested. It must be possible to test the hypothesis, or it is of little use.

Testing hypotheses that are falsifiable, that is, where it is possible to design a test that would confirm or refute the hypothesis, is at the heart of science. Thus, business model testing in this way is called a scientific approach to validation. It is scientific because it does not rest on individual whims. It relies on the evidence that the entrepreneur can muster in support of their venture.

The idea of a falsifiable hypothesis was popularized by Karl Popper, who argued it does not matter where a hypothesis comes from. As long as it is possible to devise a test that could produce a counter-example, then the hypothesis is falsifiable and, therefore, aligned with the scientific method. He said overreliance on inductive approaches leads to the proliferation of theories without an appropriate selection process to limit them to fewer, more valid theories. In the case of a business model canvas, the rejected hypotheses lead to pivots and a process of natural selection that directs the entrepreneur to more promising business models.

In this case, the hypothesis could be stated as follows: My product appeals to high-end customers. This is a testable statement that can be true or false. The relationship is between customer type (high-end versus low-end) and the appeal of a product. If a sample of more and less affluent customers rate the product and the less affluent ones find the product more attractive, then the hypothesis is rejected. If, instead, the high-end customers find appeal in the product, and the low-end customers shun it, then we have found support for our hypothesis that high-end customers will buy these products.

Similarly, in the "channels" box, the entrepreneur might write an "advertisement in Vogue Magazine with a contact phone number." Again, this is a hypothesis that the targeted customers will find the product in the magazine and call the number.

Once the entrepreneur fills out all the boxes comes the heavy lifting of customer discovery.[3] Testing each assumption or hypothesis by "getting out of the building" and asking potential customers and other stakeholders questions whose answers will either cause us to reject our hypothesis

---

[3] This is GdT. February 16, 2015. "[Great Summary] What Is Customer Discovery—Steve Blank." www.youtube.com/watch?v=vw1_-WyOtxk

or confirm it.[4] For example, if we ask high-end customers what they read and Vogue is not on the list, then that would cause us to reject our channel hypothesis. Similarly, if the high-end customers interviewed suggested they had a need or want that the envisioned product satisfied, then we might take that as support for the customer segments hypothesis.

Product Market Fit

The next step is product-market fit validation, which involves checking with the identified customers to see whether a prototype product or service solves their problem or meets the needs they expressed.

The concept of the minimal viable product (MVP) is useful here. Rather than going for a product that does everything that a selected customer segment wants, it is better to identify and develop the minimum set of features that are absolutely necessary. Achieving product-market fit means that all of the attributes of the MVP match with what the targeted customer segment wants. Misalignments should be fixed by changing the MVP.

This phase might end with preorders. Having a list of confirmed customer interests can go a long way in convincing the founders and other stakeholders of the value of scaling the venture.

Business Idea Validation for Employee Entrepreneurs

Business idea validation is a must for all entrepreneurs. However, spinouts have some advantages over de novo startups in this regard. Sometimes, business ideas have already been validated by the parent organization, often by the employees themselves.

Early Advantage

An employee might be exposed to several different stakeholders as part of their job. The role might involve interaction across different functions

---

[4] A.O. Laplume. 2021. "From Instrumental Stakeholder Theory to Stakeholder Capitalism," *Oxford Research Encyclopedia of Business and Management*.

and with external stakeholders. Employees can learn from a parent's previous investments and their results, or they may have the chance to field ideas with customers.

Feedback received within the parent organization may also be a guide. Employee entrepreneurs have the distinct advantage of being able to test hypotheses while on the job. While much of this might happen organically while working, it may also be intentional. However, intentionally testing spinout ideas may conflict with their other duties. For example, if a director were working on their startup venture during company time, this could violate fiduciary duties.

There is a relevant case where Apple litigated against a leaver, arguing that employees should not be allowed to plan their spinouts while they are still employees of the parent.[5] Taken to an extreme, a sweeping ban like this would negate nearly all spinouts.

An employee can use ordinary work experiences as a testing ground for ideas and assumptions without acting unethically. Employment puts the aspiring entrepreneur in an ideal position to pay attention to facts and trends, ask the right questions, and make astute observations.

A Head Start Canvas

Employee entrepreneurship and, especially, spinouts are different from other startups because some aspects of the business model canvas are likely already validated. That is not the case with most de novo startups.

For example, the "key activities" of the spinout may be well known, and the "value proposition" may have been previously elaborated for internal processes at the parent organization. "Key resources," especially human resources, may already be embodied in the spinout team, reducing the need to hire key human resources from the market. The spinout founder may already know about the "cost structure" related to the innovation because of internal capital budgeting exercises performed on the

---

[5] S. Nellis. Jaunary21, 2020. "Apple Lawsuit Tests If an Employee Can Plan Rival Startup While on Payroll." www.reuters.com/article/us-apple-nuvia-lawsuit/apple-lawsuit-tests-if-an-employee-can-plan-rival-startup-while-on-payroll-idINKBN1ZK16R/ (accessed December 3, 2023).

innovation. In one case we studied, the spinout founder had validated the "customer segments" while still working for the parent. They had seen that the parent organization was saying no to some customers who wanted a direct sales product. The "no" response made sense for the parent organization but not for the spinout founder, who saw an opportunity to go after that customer segment. That on-the-job experience made it possible to see the opportunity at hand. This founder explains the basis for their startup as follows:

> So I pitched the idea. I put a PowerPoint together and first we had a general dialog about it with CEO, some general discussion, and he really didn't get it, he said we don't want to get in residential. Because he was thinking of Home Depot and Walmart, and I was thinking no, instead of 10 dollars a grille, like 60 dollars a grille, that high end likes jewelry for a home, so I pitched in that way. Walmart and Home Depot products are plastic, thin, cheap and ugly but my products are designed for million dollars homes and they could never find these for their home, they go to Walmart, Home Depot and think I have to put these ugly things in my house, and now we offer them an alternative and so they might spend 3,000 dollars on their grilles whereas before they spend 100 but they hate them. So it really created a new market. (Author interview, Founder 1)

Employees in boundary-spanning roles also get to interact with different types of stakeholders that can offer clues about potential business opportunities. Opportunities are revealed through stakeholder interactions because stakeholder groups represent different networks. Understanding how the needs and abilities of different stakeholders combine to form business opportunities is at the heart of opportunity recognition.

> My colleague and I were in another country for a meeting with a big company, and they had come to [my employer] with an idea, a big idea for the two companies to partner on an important technology. They want my employer to build the payload and give it to them, so they could put it on the international space

station and we do a joint venture to sell that data. For a variety of reasons my employer wasn't crazy about this idea, it wasn't gonna work for them. But they didn't want to offend our partner in that country, because we had other good partnerships with them, so the president said to me: figure this out how to get out of this thing. So I went over there for a meeting, I had my colleague with me and we sat and talked to these guys and I had an idea so I told them forget about your idea, why don't we do something different? Why don't we put a video camera on the space station and then stream that video on the Internet, something like google earth, but movie, motion. So they liked that idea, so we came back to [my employer] and tried to do this internally [...], I did a business plan and my colleague developed some ideas about what the technology would look like.... We briefed it, I organized a meeting, I invited my boss, and the general manager of the division and I invited two or three more key senior management, and we briefed this "guy what do you think about this." [...] I presented this along with my colleague, initially some people said that's interesting and other people said it's crazy. So over time, over some months, it became obvious that this is not something that my employer really wanted to do, so I had spoken to my brother who is in a kind of venture capital, what do you think about this idea? He said it's interesting, he talked to some people and he found out that there were some angel investors who had an appetite to put about 500 thousand dollars to make the thing happen. So then he decided to found a company on this and I still was employed, the idea had no legitimacy, and he is like a guy on the street at that stage. So my employer rejected the idea, they didn't want to do it. So with management's full blessing we passed this opportunity to my brother. [...] At that point I'm in a conflict of interest for obvious reasons, so I was now removed from the project for the next little while. My colleague who is not related to my brother became my brother's supplier, so my brother put in some money and my employer now can be paid to develop the idea further and that is what happened. Several months later this idea's getting more momentum and fundamentally then I made the decision that I want to quit my job full time and go to join my brother and grow the company, so now fast forward 3.5 years from just one employee now we have about 85 employees [...] and we raised 70 million dollars and we are about to begin commercial operations in summer. (Author interview, Founder 9)

However, some degree of validation on the job does not mean that a spinout entrepreneur's whole canvas is spelt out for them; that would be a gross exaggeration even for intra-industry spinouts that imitate their parents closely. The validation process is still not complete.

Adding team members with backgrounds different from the parent company or choosing markets that are related yet different from the parent appears to be important. Research confirms that spinouts with some market knowledge overlap with their parents (but not too much) survive longer.[6] Some overlap with the parent is good, but too much decreases performance, suggesting an inverted U-shaped relationship between overlap and spinout performance. The inference is that spinouts may need to learn about new markets and networks but also unlearn some of the things they brought from their parent forms, including routines and networks that may not be optimal. In other words, do not copy the secret sauce too precisely.

There are many other tools, techniques, and training programs available to entrepreneurs. The most prominent are top startup accelerator programs like Y Combinator (YC), Techstars, and others. For example, three startups in YC's recent batch through its accelerator program are alums from Palantir. Palantir has a reputation for producing a consistent flow of spinouts, boasting over 100 alums transitioning to entrepreneurship.

In sum, spinouts have a leg up over other startups because they likely have already validated some of the assumptions that underlie their business model. This economizes resources and time.

---

[6] A. Bahoo-Torodi and S. Torrisi. 2022. "When Do Spinouts Benefit From Market Overlap With Parent Firms?" *Journal of Business Venturing* 37, no. 6, p. 106249.

About the Authors

Dr. Sepideh Yeganegi is an Associate Professor in Strategic Management at the Lazaridis School of Business and Economics, Wilfrid Laurier University in Waterloo, Canada. Her research examines employee entrepreneurship and has been published in journals such as *Research Policy* and *Journal of Small Business Management*. She has interviewed dozens of spinout founders and reviewed the growing literature on private sector employee spinouts.

Dr. André Laplume is a Professor in Entrepreneurship and Strategy at the Ted Rogers School of Management, Toronto Metropolitan University in Toronto, Canada. He researches the intersections where new entrants and incumbent firms meet with the aim of breaking down the barriers facing entrepreneurs. His research appears in *Human Relations*, *Journal of International Business Studies*, and *Journal of Business Research*.

Index

Locators followed by "*t*" in italics indicate tables.

OTHER TITLES IN THE ENTREPRENEURSHIP AND SMALL BUSINESS MANAGEMENT COLLECTION

Scott Shane, Case Western University, Editor

- *Unleashing the Startup Unicorn* by Vivek Kale
- *The Start-Up Junkie's Playbook* by Jay J. Silverberg
- *The Most Common Entrepreneurial Mistakes and How to Avoid Them* by Lisa J Peck-MacDonald
- *The Hybrid Entrepreneur* by Kevin J. Scanlon
- *Stuck Entrepreneurs* by Jay J. Silverberg
- *Teaching Old Dogs New Tricks* by Thomas Waters
- *Building Business Capacity* by Sheryl Hardin
- *The Entrepreneurial Adventure* by Oliver James
- *So, You Bought a Franchise. Now What?* by David Roemer
- *The Startup Masterplan* by Nikhil Agarwal and Krishiv Agarwal
- *Managing Health and Safety in a Small Business* by Jacqueline Jeynes
- *Modern Devil's Advocacy* by Robert Koshinskie
- *Dead Fish Don't Swim Upstream* by Jay J. Silverberg and Bruce E. McLean

Concise and Applied Business Books

The Collection listed above is one of 30 business subject collections that Business Expert Press has grown to make BEP a premiere publisher of print and digital books. Our concise and applied books are for...

- Professionals and Practitioners
- Faculty who adopt our books for courses
- Librarians who know that BEP's Digital Libraries are a unique way to offer students ebooks to download, not restricted with any digital rights management
- Executive Training Course Leaders
- Business Seminar Organizers

Business Expert Press books are for anyone who needs to dig deeper on business ideas, goals, and solutions to everyday problems. Whether one print book, one ebook, or buying a digital library of 110 ebooks, we remain the affordable and smart way to be business smart. For more information, please visit www.businessexpertpress.com, or contact sales@businessexpertpress.com.

Printed in the USA
CPSIA information can be obtained
at www.ICGtesting.com
LVHW051632301124
797961LV00002B/299